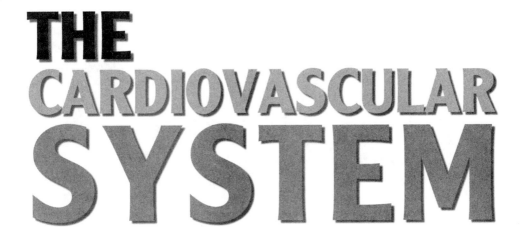

THE CARDIOVASCULAR SYSTEM

THE HUMAN BODY

THE CARDIOVASCULAR SYSTEM

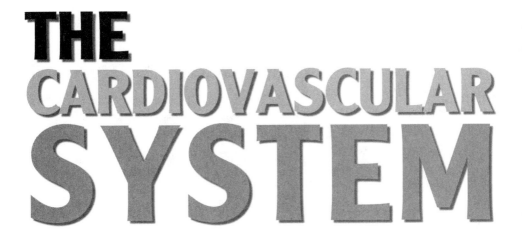

EDITED BY KARA ROGERS, SENIOR EDITOR, BIOMEDICAL SCIENCES

Britannica®
Educational Publishing

IN ASSOCIATION WITH

ROSEN
EDUCATIONAL SERVICES

Published in 2011 by Britannica Educational Publishing
(a trademark of Encyclopædia Britannica, Inc.)
in association with Rosen Educational Services, LLC
29 East 21st Street, New York, NY 10010.

First Edition

Britannica Educational Publishing
Michael I. Levy: Executive Editor
J.E. Luebering: Senior Manager
Marilyn L. Barton: Senior Coordinator, Production Control
Steven Bosco: Director, Editorial Technologies
Lisa S. Braucher: Senior Producer and Data Editor
Yvette Charboneau: Senior Copy Editor
Kathy Nakamura: Manager, Media Acquisition
Kara Rogers: Senior Editor, Biomedical Sciences

Rosen Educational Services
Hope Lourie Killcoyne: Senior Editor and Project Manager
Joanne Randolph: Editor
Nelson Sá: Art Director
Cindy Reiman: Photography Manager
Nicole Russo: Designer
Matthew Cauli: Cover Design
Introduction by Adam Chodosh, M.D.

Library of Congress Cataloging-in-Publication Data

The cardiovascular system / edited by Kara Rogers, senior editor. — 1st ed.
    p. cm. — (The human body)
"In association with Britannica Educational Publishing, Rosen Educational Services."
Includes bibliographical references and index.
ISBN 978-1-61530-128-7 (library binding)
1. Cardiovascular system. I. Rogers, Kara.
QP101.C2927 2011
612.1 — dc22

                                                    2010001624

Manufactured in the United States of America

CONTENTS

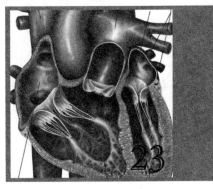

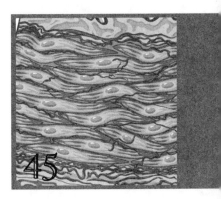
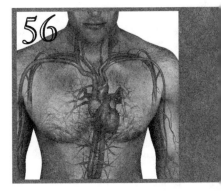

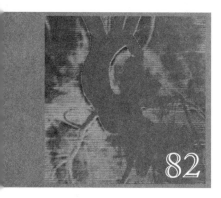

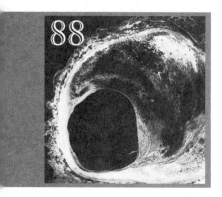

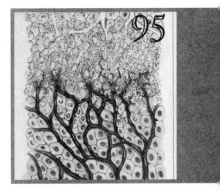

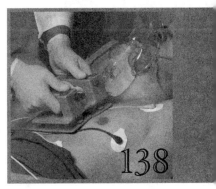

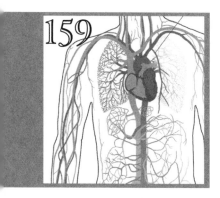

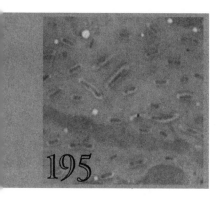

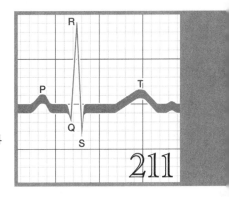

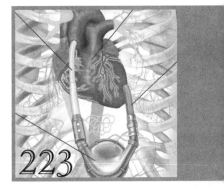

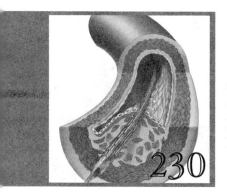

INTRODUCTION

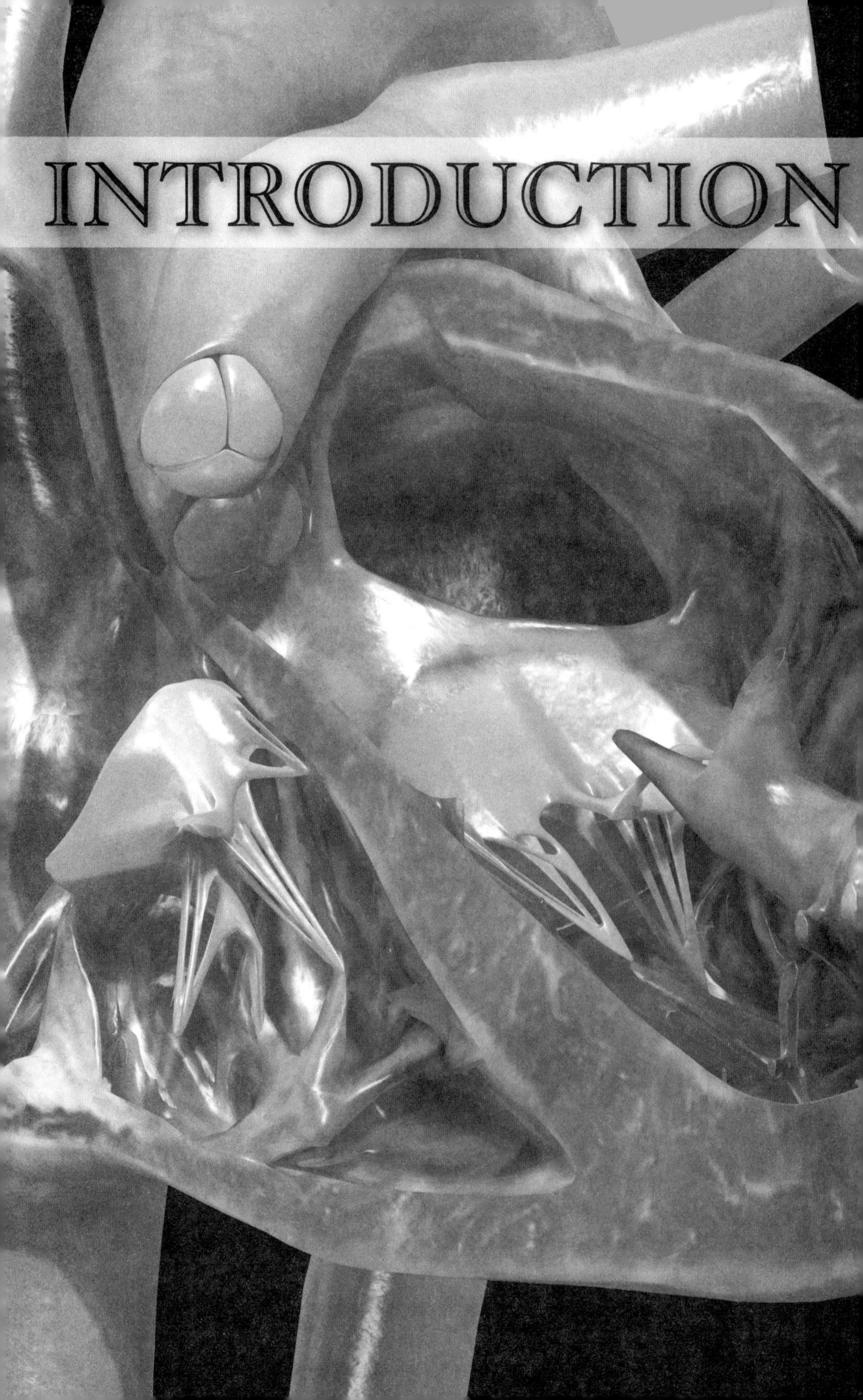

John is a 54-year-old high school AP physics teacher. One spring morning while walking his dog around the block, John developed the sudden onset of crushing chest pain. So severe was the attack that he collapsed in front of his neighbour's house. Hearing the dog's frantic barking, the neighbour rushed out, saw that John was in need of immediate medical attention, and ran to call 911. Within minutes John was taken directly to the local hospital by an ambulance. Whisked into the emergency room, a doctor performed an electrocardiogram on John, then diagnosed him as having had a myocardial infarction. (Commonly referred to as a heart attack, this is when heart muscle dies because a blocked artery causes an interruption in blood supply to the heart.) John was then quickly brought to a catheterization laboratory. There, a cardiologist threaded a small catheter into the major blood vessel leading into the blocked artery in John's heart. By inflating a tiny balloon, the doctor opened the blocked passage, thereby restoring blood flow to John's heart.

Thanks to that prompt, precise, and practiced attention, John survived, going on to do quite well after what was a near-fatal episode. Although it was a happy ending indeed, the fact that John and far too many others throughout the world suffer such attacks in the first place is a phenomenon science is working to minimize.

The accurate diagnosis and life-saving treatment that John received has evolved over hundreds of years. This volume will put into perspective the foundations of cardiac development and pathophysiology laid out by the forefathers of modern cardiology, guiding readers through the development of diagnostic and therapeutic options that exist today. In addition, the structure and function of the heart and blood vessels as well as the technologies that are used to evaluate and monitor the health of these fundamental components of the human cardiovascular system are described in detail.

The human heart, a complex organ vital to life, pumps blood throughout the body, giving the body the oxygen it needs to function properly. Normally about the size of a fist, the heart is divided into four chambers. The upper chambers, called atria, collect blood returning to the heart. They then empty the blood into the two lower chambers, called ventricles, which are the major pumping chambers of the heart.

The heart is divided into a right side and a left side. The heart's right atrium receives blood from the veins throughout the body and delivers it into the right ventricle. The right ventricle in turn pumps the blood to the lungs to pick up oxygen. The oxygen-rich blood then goes into the left atrium. Finally, the left ventricle pumps the blood through the aorta (the main artery in the body). The blood then continues on its way to all of the body organs and tissues. Four heart valves, located between each chamber, route blood flow in the proper direction. Closure of the cardiac valves produces the "lub-dub" sounds one hears when listening to the heart.

The other integral system of the heart is its ability to intrinsically conduct electricity. The electrical system is responsible for initiating and coordinating the mechanical activity of the heart. Cardiac electro-physiology is the branch of cardiology in which the electrical and arrhythmic activities of the heart are monitored, measured, studied, and treated.

Though the heart has been regarded throughout history as a vital organ, the structure and function of the cardiovascular system have nonetheless been mis-understood for a large segment of that time. The Greek physician Galen in the second century CE is credited with having first recognized that the heart and vessels contained blood rather than air, as had been taught for hundreds of years. However, Galen had no clear understanding of how blood flowed.

Galen's views endured for over a thousand years, until the early 17th century when the English physician William Harvey, through experiments based on Galen's hypotheses, established the currently accepted view of the cardiovascular system. In 1628 Harvey's *Anatomical Exercise on the Motion of the Heart and Blood in Animals* was published. In this work, he detailed how blood is pumped from the heart and through the body, and how it returns to the heart and repeats the journey all over again. Harvey's work showed that blood circulates quickly through the whole body, not just to the lungs and back as had previously been believed.

It would be another hundred years after Harvey's publication before cardiology became a specialized field of study. This occurred in 1749, when French physician Jean-Baptiste Sénac published a landmark summary of contemporary knowledge of the heart—its anatomy, physiology, and pathology. Although his two-volume text *Traité de la structure du coeur, de son action, et de ses maladies* was not limited to study of the heart, it is widely regarded as having been the first authoritative work on cardiology. Today, the medical specialty of cardiology is defined as one dealing with the diagnosis and treatment of diseases and disorders of the heart and blood vessels.

Most of the advancements in scientists' and doctors' understanding of the cardiovascular system were made simply through the power of observation. In 1772, British physician William Heberden reported a disorder in which patients developed an uncomfortable sensation in the chest upon walking. Heberden labelled it "angina pectoris." He noted that this discomfort would disappear soon after the patient stood still. Although he didn't know the cause of this sensation, his report was the first to describe the symptoms of ischemic heart disease—a lack of blood to the myocardium or heart muscle. Heart disease is a prevalent condition that now afflicts millions of people worldwide and accounts for the majority of deaths in industrialized countries.

Diseases of the heart often manifest as audible abnormalities, such as murmurs. Atypical heart sounds are clues to underlying pathophysiology. In the mid-18th century, Austrian physician Leopold Auenbrugger discovered that the condition of the lungs and heart could be estimated by the sound returned from tapping on the chest—a percussive diagnosis, as it were. This advancement was an important one of the time. That said, except in rare instances, cardiologists no longer use percussion to diagnosis heart ailments. Rather, it is the ubiquitous stethoscope that is the first step in examining the heart. This singularly simple and effective invention of French physician René-Théophile-Hyacinthe Laënnec brought the sounds of the heart directly to the ear. Initially made of a hollow wooden cylinder, this 1816 invention enabled physicians to add to their diagnostic repertoire the all-important tool of listening to heart sounds. Thereafter, physicians acquired a deeper understanding of the cardiovascular system and of heart sounds and heart murmurs through the practice called auscultation—listening to the body by way of a stethoscope. By the end of the 19th century, rubber tubing to both ears had replaced the single wooden tube.

Throughout the 19th and 20th centuries, constant improvements in diagnostic methods allowed doctors to develop a deep understanding of physiology. They gained knowledge about gas exchange in the lungs, heart muscle structure and function, congenital heart defects, electrical activity in the heart muscle, and irregular heart rhythms. One notable diagnostic advance was Dutch physiologist Willem Einthoven's 1903 invention of the electrocardiograph, a device that measures the heart's electrical activity (for this invention, he received the 1924 Nobel Prize for Physiology or Medicine). The electrocardiogram (ECG, also called an EKG after the German Elektrokardiogramm) is today easily obtained, providing a wealth of information about heart structure and function.

By the early 20th century, the basic methods for diagnosing heart disease had been established. With advances in diagnostic technology, the option of surgically correcting many heart problems became a reality. Although the study of heart anatomy dates back to ancient times, interest in the field of cardiology did not gain significant momentum until the latter half of the 20th century. At that time, the discovery and study of conditions known as congenital heart diseases—abnormalities of the heart that are present at birth—served to tremendously advance scientists' knowledge of the embryological development of the heart and of heart anatomy in neonates as well as adults.

The development of sophisticated cardiac imaging procedures such as coronary angiography (X-ray examination of the arteries and veins) and echocardiography (the generation of images of the heart by directing ultrasound waves through the chest wall) were introduced in the early 1950s. Magnetic resonance imaging (MRI) has made the spatial relationships of cardiac structures well defined, a useful step toward understanding the pathophysiology of heart disease. Other advances in cardiology during this time included the development of electrocardiographic monitors, pacemakers and defibrillators for detecting and treating arrhythmias, radio-frequency ablation of certain abnormal rhythms, balloon angioplasty (the opening of a blocked artery), and various noninvasive methods to treat otherwise complex cardiovascular diseases.

In addition to such advances, much of the development of cardiology over the course of the 20th century has been in the field of heart surgery. Major surgical advances have included the repair of coronary artery disease, one of the major causes of heart attacks. In 1923 the first successful heart-valve operation was performed on a 12-year-old girl who was suffering from a condition known as rheumatic mitral stenosis (an abnormally narrow valve). U.S. physician Elliot Cutler developed the technique, although he soon abandoned it due to the high mortality associated with the procedure. In 1967 surgeon Christiaan Barnard of South Africa performed the first human heart transplant. (Although the operation itself was a success, the patient died less than three weeks later from double pneumonia.) And in 1982, the first permanent artificial heart was surgically implanted into a patient by U.S. surgeon William C. DeVries.

This volume seeks to impart to readers a basic understanding of the human cardiovascular system. Cardiology and our comprehension of the cardiovascular system have continued to evolve in the 21st century. And it is expected that, in the coming decades, countless researchers will make discoveries in genetics and molecular biology that will further aid our understanding of cardiovascular disease and of cardiovascular health.

As for John the physics teacher, ever since his early-morning myocardial infarction, he has done very well. He exercises regularly, avoids foods with large amounts of fat and cholesterol, and subscribes to a diet rich in whole grains, nuts, fruits, and vegetables. John visits his doctors regularly, taking medications that lower his cholesterol and blood pressure, thereby reducing his risk of having a future heart attack or stroke. John has gained a profound appreciation for the team of healthcare workers that shepherded him through his crisis, the technology they relied upon, and the foundation that was laid thanks to the insight of pioneering scientists—all of which gave him his second chance. He is also grateful that his dog is a loud barker.

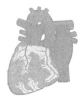

CHAPTER 1

THE HUMAN HEART

The heart is one of the most vital organs in the human body. Its function is to circulate the blood by acting as a pump. With each heartbeat, blood is pushed into the arteries and through the veins. It then courses around the body in a one-way circuit so that it eventually returns to the heart to repeat the process. Driving this constant movement of the blood are the perpetual rhythmic contractions of the heart muscle. This defining characteristic of the heart underlies the body's ability to routinely and reliably deliver oxygen and nutrients to organs, tissues, and cells.

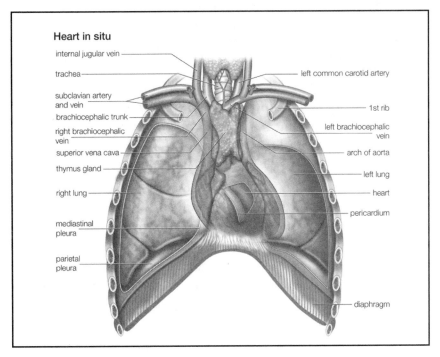

Heart in situ

internal jugular vein

trachea

subclavian artery and vein

brachiocephalic trunk

right brachiocephalic vein

superior vena cava

thymus gland

right lung

mediastinal pleura

parietal pleura

left common carotid artery

1st rib

left brachiocephalic vein

arch of aorta

left lung

heart

pericardium

diaphragm

The human heart in situ. Encyclopædia Britannica, Inc.

With the exception of some invertebrates, the heart is an anatomical feature common to members of the animal kingdom. However, the shape and complexity of the heart varies greatly among the different groups of animals. It may be a straight tube, as in spiders and annelid worms, or a somewhat more elaborate structure with one or more receiving chambers (atria) and a main pumping chamber (ventricle), as in mollusks. In fishes the heart is a folded tube, with three or four enlarged areas that correspond to the chambers in the mammalian heart. In animals with lungs—amphibians, reptiles, birds, and mammals—the heart shows various stages of evolution from a single to a double pump that circulates blood (1) to the lungs and (2) to the body as a whole.

The human adult heart is normally slightly larger than a clenched fist with average dimensions of about 13 × 9 × 6 cm (5 × 3.5 × 2.5 inches) and weighing approximately 300 grams (10.5 ounces). It is cone-shaped, with the broad base directed upward and to the right and the apex pointing downward and to the left. It is located in the chest (thoracic) cavity behind the breastbone (sternum), in front of the windpipe (trachea), the esophagus, and the descending aorta, between the lungs, and above the diaphragm. About two-thirds of the heart lies to the left of the midline.

In humans and other mammals and in birds, the heart is a four-chambered system. The heart cavity is divided down the middle into a right and a left heart, which in turn are subdivided into two chambers. The upper chamber is called an atrium, and the lower chamber is called a ventricle. The two atria act as receiving chambers for blood entering the heart. The more muscular ventricles pump the blood out of the heart.

The right atrium receives venous blood from the head, chest, and arms via the large vein called the superior vena cava and receives blood from the abdomen, pelvic region, and legs via the inferior vena cava. Blood then passes through the tricuspid valve to the right ventricle, which propels it through the pulmonary artery to the lungs. In the lungs venous blood comes in contact with inhaled air, picks up oxygen, and loses carbon dioxide. Oxygenated blood is returned to the left atrium through the pulmonary veins. Valves in the heart allow blood to flow in one direction only and help maintain the pressure required to pump the blood.

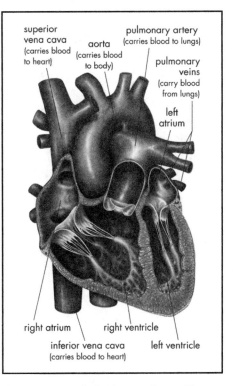

Cross section of the human heart. Encyclopædia Britannica, Inc.

The low-pressure circuit from the heart (right atrium and right ventricle), through the lungs, and back to the heart (left atrium) constitutes the pulmonary circulation. Passage of blood through the left atrium, bicuspid valve, left ventricle, aorta, tissues of the body, and back to the right atrium constitutes the systemic circulation. Blood pressure is greatest in the left ventricle and in the aorta and its arterial branches. Pressure is reduced in the capillaries (vessels of minute diameter) and is reduced further in the veins returning blood to the right atrium.

The heart consists of a tough muscular wall, the myocardium. A thin layer of tissue, the pericardium, covers the

outside of the myocardium, and another layer, the endocardium, lines the inside. The pumping of the heart, or
the heartbeat, is caused by alternating contractions and
relaxations of the myocardium.

The myocardial contractions are stimulated by electrical impulses from a natural pacemaker, the sinoatrial (or
S-A) node located in the muscle of the right atrium. An
impulse from the sinoatrial node causes the two atria to
contract, forcing blood into the ventricles. Contraction of
the ventricles is controlled by impulses from the atrioventricular (or A-V) node located at the junction of the two
atria. Following contraction, the ventricles relax, and pressure within them falls. Blood again flows into the atria, and
an impulse from the sinoatrial node starts the cycle over
again. This process is called the cardiac cycle. The period
of relaxation is called diastole. The period of contraction is
called systole. Diastole is the longer of the two phases so
that the heart can rest between contractions. In general,
the rate of heartbeat varies inversely with the size of the
animal. In elephants it averages 25 beats per minute, in
canaries about 1,000. In humans the rate diminishes progressively from birth (when it averages 130) to adolescence
but increases slightly in old age. The average adult rate is
70 beats at rest. The rate increases temporarily during
exercise, emotional excitement, and fever and decreases
during sleep. Rhythmic pulsation felt on the chest, coinciding with heartbeat, is called the apex beat. It is caused
by pressure exerted on the chest wall at the outset of systole by the rounded and hardened ventricular wall.

ORIGIN AND DEVELOPMENT

In the embryo, formation of the heart begins in the
pharyngeal, or throat, region. The first visible indication

of the embryonic heart occurs in the undifferentiated mesoderm, the middle of the three primary layers in the embryo, as a thickening of invading cells. An endocardial (lining) tube of flattened cells subsequently forms and continues to differentiate until a young tube with forked anterior and posterior ends arises. As differentiation and growth progress, this primitive tube begins to fold upon itself, and constrictions along its length produce four primary chambers. These are called, from posterior to anterior, the sinus venosus, atrium, ventricle, and truncus arteriosus. The characteristic bending of the tube causes the ventricle to swing first to the right and then behind the atrium, the truncus coming to lie between the sideways dilations of the atrium. It is during this stage of development and growth that the first pulsations of heart activity begin.

Endocardial cushions (local thickenings of the endocardium, or heart lining) "pinch" the single opening between the atrium and the ventricle into two portions, thereby forming two openings. These cushions are also responsible for the formation of the two atrioventricular valves (the valves between atria and ventricles), which regulate the direction of blood flow through the heart.

The atrium becomes separated into right and left halves first by a primary partition with a perforation and later by a secondary partition, which, too, has a large opening, called the foramen ovale, in its lower part. Even though the two openings do not quite coincide in position, blood still passes through, from the right atrium to the left. At birth, increased blood pressure in the left atrium forces the primary partition against the secondary one, so that the two openings are blocked and the atria are completely separated. The two partitions eventually fuse.

The ventricle becomes partially divided into two chambers by an indentation of myocardium (heart muscle) at its tip. This developing partition is largely muscular and is supplemented by membranous connective tissue that develops in conjunction with the subdivision of the truncus arteriosus by a spiral partition into two channels, one for systemic and one for pulmonary circulation (the aorta and the pulmonary artery, respectively). At this time, the heart rotates clockwise and to the left so that it resides in the left thorax, with the left chambers posterior and the right chambers anterior. The greater portion of blood passing through the right side of the heart in the fetus is returned to the systemic circulation by the ductus arteriosus, a vessel connecting the pulmonary artery and the aorta. At birth this duct becomes closed by a violent contraction of its muscular wall. Thereafter, the blood in the right side of the heart is driven through the pulmonary arteries to the lungs for oxygenation and returned to the left side of the heart for ejection into the systemic circulation. A distinct median furrow at the apex of the ventricles marks the external subdivision of the ventricle into right and left chambers.

PERICARDIUM

The heart is suspended in its own membranous sac, the pericardium. The strong outer portion of the sac, or fibrous pericardium, is firmly attached to the diaphragm below, the mediastinal pleura on the side, and the sternum in front. It gradually blends with the coverings of the superior vena cava and the pulmonary (lung) arteries and veins leading to and from the heart. (The space between the lungs, the mediastinum, is bordered by the mediastinal pleura, a continuation of the membrane lining the chest.

The superior vena cava is the principal channel for venous blood from the chest, arms, neck, and head.)

Smooth, serous (moisture-exuding) membrane lines the fibrous pericardium, then bends back and covers the heart. The portion of membrane lining the fibrous pericardium is known as the parietal serous layer (parietal pericardium), and the portion covering the heart is known as the visceral serous layer (visceral pericardium or epicardium).

The two layers of serous membrane are normally separated by only 10 to 15 ml (0.6 to 0.9 cubic inch) of pericardial fluid, which is secreted by the serous membranes. The slight space created by the separation is called the pericardial cavity. The pericardial fluid lubricates the two membranes with every beat of the heart as their surfaces glide over each other. Fluid is filtered into the pericardial space through both the visceral and parietal pericardia.

EXTERNAL SURFACE OF THE HEART

Shallow grooves called the interventricular sulci, containing blood vessels, mark the separation between ventricles on the front and back surfaces of the heart. There are two grooves on the external surface of the heart. One, the atrioventricular groove, is along the line where the right atrium and the right ventricle meet. It contains a branch of the right coronary artery (the coronary arteries deliver blood to the heart muscle). The other, the anterior interventricular sulcus, runs along the line between the right and left ventricles and contains a branch of the left coronary artery.

On the posterior side of the heart surface, a groove called the posterior longitudinal sulcus marks the division between the right and left ventricles. It contains another branch of a coronary artery. A fourth groove, between the left atrium and ventricle, holds the coronary sinus, a channel for venous blood.

CHAMBERS OF THE HEART

The right and left halves of the heart are divided by septa, or partitions, and each half is subdivided into two chambers, as noted previously. The upper chambers, the atria, are separated by a partition known as the interatrial septum. The lower chambers, the ventricles, are separated by the interventricular septum. The atria receive blood from various parts of the body and pass it into the ventricles. The ventricles, in turn, pump blood to the lungs and to the remainder of the body.

The right atrium, or right superior portion of the heart, is a thin-walled chamber receiving blood from all tissues except the lungs. Three veins empty into the right atrium, the superior and inferior venae cavae (previously noted), bringing blood from the upper and lower portions of the body, respectively, and the coronary sinus, draining blood from the heart itself. Blood flows from the right atrium to the right ventricle. The right ventricle, the right inferior portion of the heart, is the chamber from which the pulmonary artery carries blood to the lungs.

The left atrium, the left superior portion of the heart, is slightly smaller than the right atrium and has a thicker wall. The left atrium receives the four pulmonary veins, which bring oxygenated blood from the lungs. Blood flows from the left atrium into the left ventricle, as noted earlier. The left ventricle, the left inferior portion of the heart, has walls three times as thick as those of the right ventricle. Blood is forced from this chamber through the aorta to all parts of the body except the lungs.

ATRIA

The heart chambers that receive blood into the heart and drive it into the ventricles, the atria, have already been introduced. This section provides greater detail on the structure of these chambers. Fishes have one atrium; amphibians, reptiles, birds, and mammals have two.

In humans the atria are the two upper chambers of the heart. Each is roughly cube-shaped except for an ear-shaped projection called an auricle. (The term *auricle* is sometimes applied, incorrectly, to describe the entire atrium.) The major openings in the walls of the right atrium are (1) the points of entrance for the superior and inferior venae cavae (the great veins that return blood from the bodily tissues), and for the coronary sinus, the dilated terminal part of the cardiac vein, bearing venous blood from the heart muscle itself; and (2) the opening into the right ventricle. The principal openings into the left atrium are the points of entry of the pulmonary veins, bringing oxygenated blood from the lungs, and the opening into the left ventricle.

VENTRICLES

As discussed in earlier sections, the muscular chambers that pump blood out of the heart and into the circulatory system are known as the ventricles. Ventricles occur among some invertebrates. Among vertebrates, fishes and amphibians generally have a single ventricle, whereas reptiles, birds, and mammals have two. This section focuses on the structure of these chambers.

In humans, the ventricles are the two lower chambers of the heart. The walls of the chambers, and particularly the walls of the left ventricle, are far more heavily muscled than the walls of the atria because it is in the ventricles that the major force is exerted in the process of pumping the blood to the bodily tissues and to the lungs. Each opening leading into or away from the ventricles is guarded by a valve. These openings are the following: those from the two upper chambers; the opening from the right ventricle into the pulmonary artery, which transports blood to the lungs; and the opening from the left ventricle into the aorta, the main trunk by which oxygen-rich blood starts its course to the tissues. The interior surfaces of the ventricles are ridged with bundles and bands of muscle, called trabeculae carneae. The papillary muscles project like nipples into the cavities of the ventricles. They are attached by fine strands of tendon to the valves between the atria and ventricles and prevent the valves from opening when the ventricles contract.

VALVES OF THE HEART

To prevent backflow of blood, the heart is equipped with valves that permit the blood to flow in only one direction. There are two types of valves located in the heart: the atrioventricular valves (tricuspid and mitral) and the semilunar valves (pulmonary and aortic).

The atrioventricular valves are thin, leaflike structures located between the atria and the ventricles. The right atrioventricular opening is guarded by the tricuspid valve, so called because it consists of three irregularly shaped cusps, or flaps. The leaflets consist essentially of folds of endocardium (the membrane lining the heart) reinforced with a flat sheet of dense connective tissue. At the base of the leaflets, the middle supporting flat plate becomes continuous with that of the dense connective tissue of the ridge surrounding the openings.

Tendinous cords of dense tissue (chordae tendineae) covered by thin endocardium extend from the nipplelike papillary muscles to connect with the ventricular surface of the middle supporting layer of each leaflet. The chordae tendineae and the papillary muscles from which they arise limit the extent to which the portions of the valves near their free margin can billow toward the atria. The left atrioventricular opening is guarded by the mitral, or bicuspid, valve, so named because it consists of two flaps. The mitral valve is attached in the same manner as the tricuspid, but it is stronger and thicker because the left ventricle is by nature a more powerful pump working under high pressure.

Blood is propelled through the tricuspid and mitral valves as the atria contract. When the ventricles contract, blood is forced backward, passing between the flaps and walls of the ventricles. The flaps are thus pushed upward until they meet and unite, forming a complete partition between the atria and the ventricles. The expanded flaps of the valves are restrained by the chordae tendineae and papillary muscles from opening into the atria.

The semilunar valves are pocketlike structures attached at the point at which the pulmonary artery and the aorta leave the ventricles. The pulmonary valve guards the orifice between the right ventricle and the pulmonary artery. The aortic valve protects the orifice between the left ventricle and the aorta. The three leaflets of the aortic semilunar and two leaflets of the pulmonary valves are thinner than those of the atrioventricular valves, but they are of the same general construction with the exception that they possess no chordae tendineae.

Closure of the heart valves is associated with an audible sound, called the heartbeat. The first sound occurs when the mitral and tricuspid valves close, the second when the pulmonary and aortic semilunar valves close.

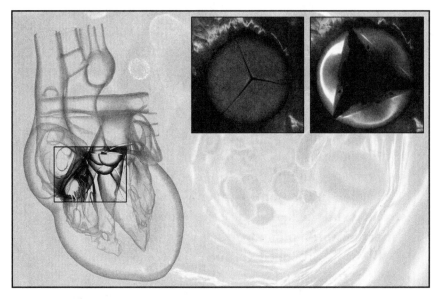

This pull-out view shows an open and a closed tricuspid valve, which is also called the right atrioventricular valve due to its location between the right atrium and ventricle. 3D4Medical.com/Getty Images

THE HEART WALL

As noted in the first section of this chapter, the wall of the heart consists of three distinct layers—the epicardium (outer layer), the myocardium (middle layer), and the endocardium (inner layer). Coronary vessels supplying arterial blood to the heart penetrate the epicardium before entering the myocardium. This outer layer, or visceral pericardium, consists of a surface of flattened epithelial (covering) cells resting upon connective tissue.

The myocardial layer contains the contractile elements of the heart. The bundles of striated muscle fibres present in the myocardium are arranged in a branching pattern and produce a wringing type of movement that efficiently squeezes blood from the heart with each beat. The thickness of the myocardium varies according to the pressure generated to move blood to its destination. The myocardium of the left ventricle, which must drive blood out into the systemic circulation, is, therefore, thickest. The myocardium of the right ventricle, which propels blood to the lungs, is moderately thickened, while the atrial walls are relatively thin.

The component of the myocardium causing contraction consists of muscle fibres that are made up of cardiac muscle cells. Each cell contains smaller fibres known as myofibrils that house highly organized contractile units called sarcomeres. The mechanical function arising from sarcomeres is produced by specific contractile pro-

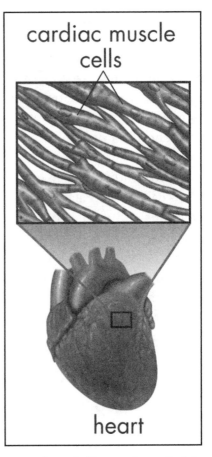

Striated muscle fibres in the wall of the heart. Encyclopædia Britannica, Inc.

teins known as actin and myosin (or thin and thick filaments, respectively). The sarcomere, found between two Z lines (or Z discs) in a muscle fibre, contains two populations of actin filaments that project from opposite Z lines in antiparallel fashion and are organized around thick filaments of myosin. As actin slides along crossbridges that project from myosin filaments at regular intervals, each myosin is brought into contact with an adjacent myosin filament. This process shortens the muscle fibre and causes contraction.

Interaction between actin and myosin is regulated by a variety of biological processes that are generally related to the concentration of calcium within the cell. The process of actin sliding over myosin requires large amounts of both calcium and energy. While the contractile machinery occupies about 70 percent of the cardiac cell volume, mitochondria occupy about 25 percent and provide the necessary energy for contraction. To facilitate energy and calcium conductance in cardiac muscle cells, unique junctions called intercalated discs (gap junctions) link the cells together and define their borders. Intercalated discs are the major portal for cardiac cell-to-cell communication, which is required for coordinated muscle contraction and maintenance of circulation.

Forming the inner surface of the myocardial wall is a thin lining called the endocardium. This layer lines the cavities of the heart, covers the valves and small muscles associated with opening and closing of the valves, and is continuous with the lining membrane of the large blood vessels.

BLOOD SUPPLY TO THE HEART

Because of the watertight lining of the heart (the endocardium) and the thickness of the myocardium, the heart cannot depend on the blood contained in its own chambers for oxygen and nourishment. It possesses a vascular system of its own, called the coronary arterial system. In the most common distribution, this comprises two major coronary arteries, the right and the left. Normally, the left coronary artery divides soon after its origin into two major branches, called the left anterior descending and the circumflex coronary arteries. The right, the left anterior descending, and the left circumflex coronary arteries have many branches and are of almost equal importance. Thus, there are commonly said to be three main functional coronary arteries rather than two.

The right and left coronary arteries originate from the right and left aortic sinuses (the sinuses of Valsalva), which are bulges at the origin of the ascending aorta immediately beyond, or distal to, the aortic valve. The ostium, or opening, of the right coronary artery is in the right aortic sinus and that of the left coronary artery is in the left aortic sinus, just above the aortic valve ring. There is also a non-coronary sinus of Valsalva, which lies to the left and posteriorly at the origin of the ascending aorta. The left coronary arterial system is more important than the right because it supplies blood to the larger left ventricle, and the dimension of the left coronary ostium is larger than that of the right.

The right coronary artery has a lumen diameter of about 2.5 mm (about 0.1 inch) or more. It supplies the right ventricular outflow tract, the sinoatrial node (the principal pacemaker of the heart), the atrioventricular node, and the bulk of the right ventricle, with branches extending into the interventricular septum and joining with arteriolar branches from the left coronary artery more or less where the two ventricles join.

The main stem of the left coronary artery has a lumen diameter often exceeding 4.5 mm (about 0.2 inch) and is one of the shortest and most important vessels of the body. Usually, it is between 1 and 2 cm (about 0.4 and 0.8 inch) in length, but it may have a length of only 2 mm (0.08 inch) before dividing. Sometimes the main left coronary artery may actually be missing, with the left coronary ostium having two separate openings for the left anterior descending and the left circumflex arteries. The main left coronary artery divides into its two branches, the anterior descending and the circumflex, while still in the space between the aorta and pulmonary artery. The left anterior descending coronary artery usually begins as a continuation of the left main coronary artery, and its size, length, and distribution are key factors in the balance of the supply of blood to the left ventricle and the interventricular septum. There are many branches of the left anterior descending artery. The first and usually the largest septal branch is important because of its prominent role in supplying blood to the septum.

The left circumflex artery leaves the left main coronary artery to run posteriorly along the atrioventricular groove. It divides soon after its origin into an atrial branch and an obtuse marginal branch. The former branch sometimes has a branch to the sinoatrial node (more usually supplied from the right coronary artery). The obtuse marginal vessel supplies the posterior left ventricular wall in the direction of the apex.

Venous blood from the heart is carried through veins, which usually accompany the distribution of the distal arteries. These cardiac veins, however, proceed into the atrioventricular grooves anteriorly and posteriorly to form the coronary venous sinus, which opens into the right ventricle immediately below the tricuspid valve.

In addition to these identifiable anatomic arterial and venous channels, nutritional exchange almost certainly takes place between the endocardial ventricular muscle layers and the blood in the cavity of the ventricles. This is of minor importance and probably is an adaptive system in situations of cardiac muscle pathology.

HEARTBEAT

Regular beating of the heart is achieved as a result of the inherent rhythmicity of cardiac muscle. No nerves are located within the heart itself, and no outside regulatory mechanisms are necessary to stimulate the muscle to contract rhythmically. That these rhythmic contractions originate in the cardiac muscle can be substantiated by observing cardiac development in the embryo where cardiac pulsations begin before adequate development of nerve fibres. In addition, it can be demonstrated in the laboratory that even fragments of cardiac muscle in tissue culture continue to contract rhythmically. Furthermore, there is no gradation in degree of contraction of the muscle fibres of the heart, as would be expected if they were primarily under nervous control.

THE CONDUCTION SYSTEM

The mere possession of an intrinsic ability to contract is not sufficient, however, to enable the heart to function efficiently. Proper function requires coordination, which is maintained by an elaborate conducting system within the heart that consists primarily of two small, specialized masses of tissue, or nodes, from which impulses originate, and of nervelike conduits for the transmission of impulses, with terminal branches extending to the inner surface of the ventricles.

Rhythmic cardiac contractions originate with an electrical impulse that travels from the top of the heart in the atria to the bottom of the heart in the ventricles. The impulse is propagated as a wave that travels from cell to cell. Voltage-sensitive protein channels on the surface of the sarcolemma, the membrane that surrounds the muscle fibre, support the flow of current as it relates to the flow of specific ions (ion-specific channels). These voltage-sensitive channels open and close as a function of the voltage that is sensed on the outer side and inner side (referred to as being "across the membrane," or transmembrane) of the sarcolemma, between which a difference in electrical potential exists. An electrical potential gradient is created by an excess of negative ions immediately inside the sarcolemma and an equal excess of positive ions on the outside of the sarcolemma (a stage known as the resting potential). When a nerve impulse stimulates ion channels to open, positive ions flow into the cell and cause depolarization, which leads to muscle cell contraction.

Under resting conditions the heart cell is primarily permeable only to positively charged potassium ions, which slowly leak into the cell. In specialized pacemaking cells, found in the sinoatrial node, the negative resting potential rhythmically drifts toward the positive threshold potential. When the threshold potential is exceeded, depolarization of the cell is triggered, and there is an opening of ion channels that transport sodium and calcium into the cell. This sudden increase in cardiac membrane potential is transmitted from cell to cell, creating a wave of depolarization that functionally represents the excitation signal of the heart. Propagation of the signal rapidly progresses down conduction tissue via specialized atrial cells, the atrioventricular node, and the bundles of His and Purkinje cells and is followed by a slower dispersion of the signal in ventricular muscle cells. The rate of spontaneous depolarization is an important determinant of heart rate.

Both the excitation and propagation mechanisms are sensitive to alterations in the ion concentration of the extracellular and intracellular fluid, as well as drugs that might alter the carriers or channels associated with these ions. Following the initial depolarization event in cardiac muscle cells, there is a sequence of openings and closures of specific channels that ultimately result in a return to the resting transmembrane potential. This highly orchestrated interaction of different voltage-sensitive channels, and the resultant changes in transmembrane voltage, is called the cardiac action potential.

The depolarization event in the cardiac muscle cell also opens a calcium channel, allowing calcium to enter the myocardium. Calcium is an important effector of the coupling between cardiac depolarization (excitation) and cardiac contraction (called "excitation-contraction coupling"). Under normal circumstances, free calcium ion concentration in the cardiac muscle cell is very low. This low concentration is maintained by the presence of an internal membrane system called the sarcoplasmic reticulum that sequesters calcium ions. Upon excitation and depolarization of the cell, the calcium channel opens and admits a small amount of calcium associated with the shift in the membrane potential. This small amount of calcium stimulates the release of additional calcium from calcium-sensitive channels in the sarcoplasmic reticulum, causing the cellular calcium concentration to rise by nearly 100-fold. When the heart is repolarized, the sarcoplasmic reticulum reabsorbs the excess calcium, and the cellular calcium concentration returns to its formerly low level, letting the heart muscle relax.

Reabsorption of cellular calcium by the sarcoplasmic reticulum is important because it prevents the development of muscle tension. In the resting state, two proteins, troponin and tropomyosin, bind to actin molecules and inhibit interaction between actin and myosin, thereby blocking muscle contraction. When calcium concentration increases during depolarization, it shifts the conformation of troponin and tropomyosin, and actin is able to associate with myosin. As calcium is taken up again by the sarcoplasmic reticulum the myocardial cell relaxes. Factors that control the rise and fall of calcium concentrations in the cardiac muscle cell have profound effects on heart function.

Nervous Control of the Heart

Nervous control of the heart is maintained by the parasympathetic fibres in the vagus nerve and by the sympathetic nerves. The vagus nerve acts as a cardiac inhibitor, and the sympathetic nerves serve as cardiac excitors. Stimulation of the vagus nerve depresses the rate of impulse formation and atrial contractility and thereby reduces cardiac output and slows the rate of the heart. Parasympathetic stimulation can also produce varying degrees of impaired impulse formation or heart block in diseases of the heart. (In complete heart block the atria and the ventricles beat independently.) Stimulation of the sympathetic nerves increases contractility of both atria and ventricles.

The cardiac cycle is defined as the time from the end of one heart contraction to the end of the subsequent contraction and, as already mentioned, consists of a period of relaxation called diastole followed by a period of contraction called systole. During the entire cycle, pressure is maintained in the arteries. However, this pressure varies during the two periods, the normal diastolic pressure being 60 to 80 mmHg ("millimetres of mercury") and the normal systolic pressure being 90 to 120 mmHg.

Cardiac Output

Cardiac output is the volume of blood expelled by either ventricle of the heart. It is customarily expressed as minute volume, or litres of blood per minute, calculated as the product of stroke volume (output of either ventricle per heartbeat) and the number of beats per minute. Maintaining and regulating cardiac output, which is usually proportional to the tissues' need for oxygen and other nutrients, is one of the circulatory system's most intricate functions. In the healthy human adult, resting (or basal) output is estimated to be slightly over 5 litres (5.3 quarts) per minute. Normally, it decreases somewhat when a person changes from recumbent to upright position. It may be increased 50 to 100 percent by anxiety and excitement and as much as fivefold by exercise. Measurement of cardiac output, as first described by German physiologist Adolf E. Fick in 1870, makes possible an evaluation of respiratory exchange (i.e., the delivery of oxygen to the tissues).

SYSTOLE AND DIASTOLE

As noted, the period of contraction of the ventricles of the heart is known as systole. Systole causes the ejection of blood into the aorta and pulmonary trunk. Lasting usually 0.3 to 0.4 second, ventricular systole is introduced by a very brief period of contraction, followed by the ejection phase, during which 80 to 100 cubic centimetres (5–6 cubic inches) of blood leave each ventricle. During systole, arterial blood pressure reaches its peak (systolic blood pressure), normally about 90 to 120 mmHg in humans. This is slightly lower than the ventricular pressure because of the distensibility of the vessel walls. Atrial systole occurs toward the end of ventricular diastole, completing the filling of the ventricles.

As also noted, diastole is the period of relaxation of the heart muscle in the cardiac cycle and is accompanied by the filling of the chambers with blood. Initially both atria and ventricles are in diastole, and there is a period of rapid filling of the ventricles followed by a brief atrial systole. At the same time, there is a corresponding decrease in arterial blood pressure to its minimum (diastolic blood pressure), normally about 80 mmHg in humans. Ventricular diastole again occurs after the blood has been ejected (during ventricular systole) into the aorta and pulmonary artery.

HEART SOUNDS AND MURMURS

The rhythmic noises accompanying the heartbeat are called heart sounds. Normally, two distinct sounds are heard through the stethoscope: a low, slightly prolonged "lub" (first sound) occurring at the beginning of systole, and a sharper, higher-pitched "dup" (second sound), occurring at the end of systole. These characteristic heart sounds have been found to be caused by the vibration of the walls of the heart and major vessels around the heart. The low-frequency first heart sound is heard when the ventricles contract, causing a sudden backflow of blood that closes the valves and causes them to bulge back. The elasticity of the valves then causes the blood to bounce backward into each respective ventricle. This effect sets the walls of the ventricles into vibration, and the vibrations travel away from the valves. When the vibrations reach the chest wall where the wall is in contact with the heart, sound waves are created that can be heard with the aid of a stethoscope.

The second heart sound results from vibrations set up in the walls of the pulmonary artery, the aorta, and, to a lesser extent, the ventricles, as the blood reverberates back and forth between the walls of the arteries and the valves after the pulmonary and aortic semilunar valves suddenly close. These vibrations are then heard as a high-frequency sound as the chest wall transforms the vibrations into sound waves. The first heart sound is followed after a short pause by the second. A pause about twice as long comes between the second sound and the beginning of the next cycle. The opening of the valves is silent.

Occasionally audible in normal hearts is a third soft, low-pitched sound coinciding with early diastole and thought to be produced by vibrations of the ventricular wall. A fourth sound, also occurring during diastole, is revealed by graphic methods but is usually inaudible in normal subjects. It is believed to be the result of atrial contraction and the impact of blood, expelled from the atria, against the ventricular wall.

Heart "murmurs" may be readily heard by a physician as soft swishing or hissing sounds that follow the normal sounds of heart action. Murmurs may indicate that blood is leaking through an imperfectly closed valve and may signal the presence of a serious heart problem.

CHAPTER 2

THE BLOOD VESSELS

The blood vessels consist of a closed system of tubes that transport blood to all parts of the body and back to the heart. The major types of vessels include the arteries, veins, and capillaries. As in any biologic system, structure and function of the vessels are so closely related that one cannot be discussed without the other's being taken into account.

Because of the need for the early development of a transport system within the embryo, the organs of the vascular system are among the first to appear and to assume their functional role. In fact, this system is established in its basic form by the fourth week of embryonic life. At approximately the 18th day of gestation, cells begin to group together between the outer skin (ectoderm) and the inner skin (endoderm) of the embryo. These cells soon become rearranged so that the more peripheral ones join to form a continuous flattened sheet enclosing more centrally placed cells. These cells remain suspended in a fluid medium as primitive blood cells. The tubes then expand and unite to form a network; the primitive blood vessels thus appear.

In the human body, there exist discrete systems of vessels that perform very specific functions while also contributing to the overall circulation of blood. The portal system, for example, consists of a network of vessels and is specially designed to transport blood from the abdomen to the liver, where nutrients, wastes, and other substances that have been absorbed from the gastrointestinal tract are metabolized. The processed blood then leaves the liver and travels to the heart. Two other readily distinguished systems are the pulmonary circulation, which is a closed network of vessels that supplies blood only to the heart and lungs, and the systemic circulation, which supplies blood to tissues throughout the body.

ARTERIES

Arteries are any of the vessels that, with one exception, carry oxygenated blood and nourishment from the heart

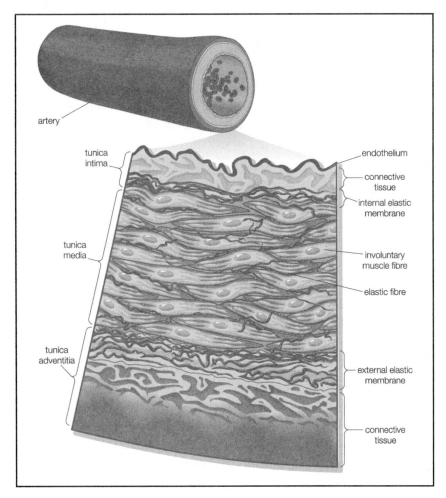

Transverse section of an artery. Encyclopædia Britannica, Inc.

to the tissues of the body. The exception, the pulmonary artery, carries oxygen-depleted blood to the lungs for oxygenation and removal of excess carbon dioxide.

Arteries transport blood to body tissues under high pressure, which is exerted by the pumping action of the heart. The heart forces blood into the elastic tubes, which recoil, sending blood on in pulsating waves. The pulse, which can be felt over an artery lying near the surface of the skin, results from the alternate expansion and contraction of the arterial wall as the beating heart forces blood into the arterial system via the aorta. Large arteries branch off from the aorta and in turn give rise to smaller arteries until the level of the smallest arteries, or arterioles, is reached. The threadlike arterioles carry blood to networks of microscopic capillaries, which supply nourishment and oxygen to the tissues and carry away carbon dioxide and other products of metabolism by way of the veins.

Because the blood is pushed through the arteries at high pressure, it is imperative that the vessels possess strong, elastic walls. These features also ensure that the blood flows quickly and efficiently to the tissues. The wall of an artery consists of three layers. The tunica intima, the innermost layer, consists of an inner surface of smooth endothelium covered by a surface of elastic tissues. The tunica media, or middle coat, is thicker in arteries, particularly in the large arteries, and consists of smooth muscle cells intermingled with elastic fibres. The muscle cells and elastic fibres circle the vessel. In larger vessels the tunica media is composed primarily of elastic fibres. As arteries become smaller, the number of elastic fibres decreases while the number of smooth muscle fibres increases. The tunica adventitia, the outermost layer, is the strongest of the three layers. It is composed of collagenous and elastic fibres. (Collagen is a connective-tissue protein.) The tunica adventitia provides a limiting barrier, protecting the vessel from overexpansion. Also characteristic of this layer is the presence of small blood vessels called the vasa vasorum that supply the walls of larger arteries and veins. In contrast, the inner and middle layers are nourished by diffusion from the blood as it is transported. The thicker, more elastic wall of arteries enables them to expand with the pulse and to regain their original size.

The transition from artery to arteriole is a gradual one, marked by a progressive thinning of the vessel wall and a decrease in the size of the lumen, or passageway. In arterioles, the tunica intima is still present as a lining covered by a layer of thin longitudinal fibres. However, the tunica media no longer contains elastic fibres and is composed of only a single layer of circular or spiral smooth muscle fibres. The tunica adventitia consists of connective tissue elements.

The small arteries and arterioles act as control valves through which blood is released into the capillaries. The strong muscular wall is capable of closing the passageway or permitting it to expand to several times its normal size, thereby vastly altering blood flow to the capillaries. Blood flow is by this device directed to tissues that require it most.

As the arterioles become smaller in size, the three coats become less and less definite, with the smallest arterioles consisting of little more than endothelium, or lining, surrounded by a layer of smooth muscle. The microscopic capillary tubules consist of a single layer of endothelium that is a continuation of the innermost lining cells of arteries and veins.

As the capillaries converge, small venules are formed whose function it is to collect blood from the capillary beds (i.e., the networks of capillaries). The venules consist of an endothelial tube supported by a small amount of collagenous tissue and, in the larger venules, by a few smooth muscle fibres as well. As venules continue to increase in size, they begin to exhibit wall structure that is characteristic of arteries, though they are much thinner.

THE AORTA AND ITS PRINCIPAL BRANCHES

The aorta is the largest artery and is the vessel responsible for carrying blood from the heart to all the organs and other structures of the body. The aorta arises from the left ventricle, and at the opening where these two structures connect there is a three-part valve that prevents the back-flow of blood from the vessel into the heart.

The aorta is commonly said to have three regions: the ascending aorta, the arch of the aorta, and the descending aorta. The latter may be further subdivided into the thoracic and the abdominal aorta. The ascending aorta emerges from the left ventricle and then turns to the left, arches over the heart (the aortic arch), and passes downward as the descending aorta.

Originating from the ascending portion of the aorta are the right and left coronary arteries, which supply the heart with oxygenated blood. Branching from the arch of the aorta are three large arteries named, in order of origin from the heart, the innominate, the left common carotid, and the left subclavian. These three branches supply the head, neck, and arms with oxygenated blood.

As the innominate (sometimes referred to as the brachiocephalic) artery travels upward toward the clavicle, or collarbone, it divides into the right common carotid and right subclavian arteries. The two common carotid arteries, one branching from the innominate and the other directly from the aorta, then extend in a parallel fashion on either side of the neck to the top of the thyroid cartilage (the principal cartilage in the voice box, or larynx), where they divide, each to become an internal and an external carotid artery. The external carotid arteries give off branches that supply much of the head and neck, while the internal carotids are responsible for supplying the forward portion of the brain, the eye and its appendages, and the forehead and nose.

The two vertebral arteries, one arising as a branch of the innominate and the other as a branch of the left subclavian artery, unite at the base of the brain to form the basilar artery, which in turn divides into the posterior cerebral arteries. The blood supply to the brain is derived mainly from vessels that may be considered as branches of the circle of Willis, which is made up of the two vertebral and the two internal carotid arteries and connecting arteries between them.

The arms are supplied by the subclavian artery on the left and by the continuation of the innominate on the right. At approximately the border of the first rib, both of these vessels become known as the axillary artery. This, in turn, becomes the brachial artery as it passes down the upper arm. At about the level of the elbow, the brachial artery divides into two terminal branches, the radial and ulnar arteries, the radial passing downward on the distal (thumb) side of the forearm, the ulnar on the medial side. Interconnections (anastomoses) between the two, with branches at the level of the palm, supply the hand and wrist.

As the aorta descends along the backbone, it gives rise to major arteries that supply the internal organs of the thorax (chest). The thoracic branches of the aorta supply the viscera (visceral branches) and the walls surrounding the thoracic cavity (parietal branches). The visceral branches provide blood for the pericardium, lungs, bronchi, lymph nodes, and esophagus. The parietal vessels supply the intercostal muscles (the muscles between the ribs) and the muscles of the thoracic wall. They supply blood to the membrane covering the lungs and lining the thoracic cavity, the spinal cord, the vertebral column, and a portion of the diaphragm.

As the aorta descends through the diaphragm, it becomes known as the abdominal aorta and again gives off both visceral and parietal branches. Visceral vessels include the celiac, superior mesenteric, and inferior mesenteric, which are unpaired, and the renal and testicular or ovarian, which are paired. The celiac artery arises from the aorta a short distance below the diaphragm and almost immediately divides into the left gastric artery, serving part of the stomach and esophagus; the hepatic artery, which primarily serves the liver; and the splenic artery, which supplies the stomach, pancreas, and spleen.

The superior mesenteric artery arises from the abdominal aorta just below the celiac artery. Its branches supply the small intestine and part of the large intestine. Arising several centimetres above the termination of the aorta is the inferior mesenteric artery, which branches to supply the lower part of the colon. The renal arteries pass to the kidneys. The testicular or ovarian arteries supply the testes in the male and the ovaries in the female, respectively.

Parietal branches of the abdominal aorta include the inferior phrenic, serving the suprarenal (adrenal) glands, the lumbar, and the middle sacral arteries. The lumbar arteries are arranged in four pairs and supply the muscles of the abdominal wall, the skin, the lumbar vertebrae, the spinal cord, and the meninges (spinal-cord coverings).

The abdominal aorta divides into two common iliac arteries, each of which descends laterally and gives rise to external and internal branches. The right and left external iliac arteries are direct continuations of the common iliacs and become known as the femoral arteries after passing through the inguinal region, giving off branches that supply structures of the abdomen and lower extremities.

At a point just above the knee, the femoral artery continues as the popliteal artery. From this arise the posterior and anterior tibial arteries. The posterior tibial artery is a direct continuation of the popliteal, passing down the lower leg to supply structures of the posterior portion of the leg and foot.

Arising from the posterior tibial artery a short distance below the knee is the peroneal artery. This gives off branches that nourish the lower leg muscles and the fibula (the smaller of the two bones in the lower leg) and terminate in the foot. The anterior tibial artery passes down the lower leg to the ankle, where it becomes the dorsalis pedis artery, which supplies the foot.

Renal Artery

There are two renal arteries in the human body. As mentioned briefly ealier, these large vessels branch off from the abdominal aorta and enter into each kidney. The kidneys, a pair of bean-shaped organs, serve to remove waste substances from the blood and aid in fluid conservation and in stabilization of the chemical composition of the blood. At the inner concavity of each kidney there is an opening, known as the hilum, through which the renal artery passes. After passing through the hilum, the renal artery divides ordinarily into two large branches, and each branch divides into a number of smaller arteries, which bring blood to the nephrons, the functioning units of the kidney. Blood that has been processed by the nephrons ultimately reaches the renal vein, which carries it back to the inferior vena cava and to the right side of the heart.

The renal arteries deliver to the kidneys of a normal person at rest 1.2 litres (2.5 pints) of blood per minute, a volume equivalent to approximately one-quarter of the heart's output. Thus, a volume of blood equal to all that found in the body of an adult human is processed by the kidneys once every four to five minutes. Although some physical conditions can inhibit blood flow, there are certain self-regulatory mechanisms inherent to the arteries of the kidney that allow some adaptation to stress. When the total body blood pressure rises or drops, sensory receptors of the nervous system located in the smooth muscle wall of the arteries are affected by the pressure changes, and, to compensate for the blood pressure variations, the arteries either expand or contract to keep a constant volume of blood flow.

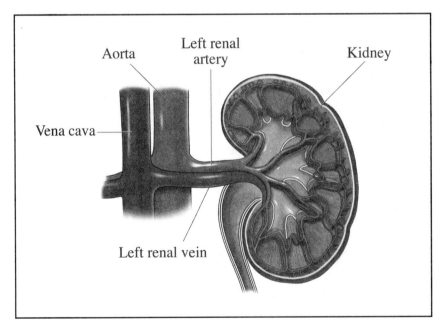

This diagram illustrates the arterial and venous blood supply to the kidneys.
Nucleus Medical Art, Inc./Getty Images

THE PULSE

The pulse is the rhythmic dilation of an artery. The pulse is generated by the opening and closing of the aortic valve in the heart, which reflects the alternate expansion and contraction of the arterial wall that is driven by the beating of the heart. When the heart pushes blood into the aorta, the blood's impact on the elastic walls creates a pressure wave that continues along the arteries. This impact is the pulse. All arteries have a pulse, but it is most easily felt at points where the vessel approaches the surface of the body.

The association of pulse with the action of the heart was recognized by the ancient Egyptians, and it remains a valuable indicator of cardiac function in modern medicine. Pulse rate, strength, and rhythm all provide valuable diagnostic information. For example, the regular alteration between strong and weak pulses can indicate heart failure. A rapid pulse may indicate serious cardiac disease, a relatively innocuous fever, or simply vigorous exercise. A slow pulse may be a result of head injury, but it is also normal in highly trained athletes with exceptional heart function.

A pulse can be felt by applying firm fingertip pressure to the skin at sites where the arteries travel near the skin's surface. It is more evident when surrounding muscles are relaxed. The pulse is readily distinguished at the following locations: (1) at the point in the wrist where the radial artery approaches the surface; (2) at the side of the lower jaw where the external maxillary (facial) artery crosses it; (3) at the temple above and to the outer side of the eye, where the temporal artery is near the surface; (4) on the side of the neck, from the carotid artery; (5) on the inner side of the biceps, from the brachial artery; (6) in the groin, from the femoral artery; (7) behind the knee, from the popliteal artery; and (8) on the upper side of the foot, from the dorsalis pedis artery.

The radial artery is most commonly used to check the pulse. Several fingers are placed on the artery close to the wrist joint. More than one fingertip is preferable because of the large, sensitive surface available to feel the pulse wave. While the pulse is being checked, certain data are recorded, including the number and regularity of beats per minute, the force and strength of the beat, and the tension offered by the artery to the finger. Normally, the interval between beats is of equal length.

Pulse rates vary from person to person. The normal pulse rate of an adult at rest may range from 50 to 85 beats per minute, although the average rate is about 70 to 72 for men and 78 to 82 for women. In infants the rate ranges from 110 to 140. The rate decreases with age, and the rate for adolescents is 80 to 90. The normal rate for the elderly may be 50 to 70.

VEINS

Veins are any of the vessels that, with four exceptions, carry oxygen-depleted blood to the right upper atrium of the heart. The four exceptions—the pulmonary veins—transport oxygenated blood from the lungs to the left upper chamber of the heart.

The oxygen-depleted blood transported by most veins is collected from capillary networks by thread-sized veins called venules. Venules also collect blood from channels known as sinusoids. Venules unite to form progressively larger veins that terminate as the great veins, or venae cavae. There are two great veins: the superior vena cava, which delivers blood from the upper body to the right atrium of the heart, and the inferior vena cava, which delivers blood from the lower body to the right atrium. Venous blood can also enter the right atrium from the heart muscle itself, by way of the coronary sinus.

In the extremities, there are superficial and deep veins. The superficial veins lie just under the skin and drain the skin and superficial fasciae (sheets of fibrous tissue), while the deep veins accompany the principal arteries of the extremities and are similarly named. Interconnections between the superficial and the deep veins are frequent.

As in the arteries, the walls of veins have three layers, or coats: an inner layer, or tunica intima; a middle layer, or tunica media; and an outer layer, or tunica adventitia. Each coat has a number of sublayers. The tunica intima differs from the inner layer of an artery: many veins, particularly in the arms and legs, have valves to prevent backflow of blood, and the elastic membrane lining the artery is absent in the vein, which consists primarily of endothelium and scant connective tissue. The tunica media, which in an artery is composed of muscle and elastic fibres, is thinner in a vein and contains less muscle and elastic tissue, and proportionately more collagen fibres. The outer layer, the tunica adventitia, consists chiefly of connective tissue and is the thickest layer of the vein. As in arteries, there are tiny vessels called vasa vasorum that supply blood to the walls of the veins and other minute vessels that carry blood away.

Since the walls of veins are constructed in such a way as to enable them to expand or contract, they are more distensible than arteries. A major function of their contractility appears to be to decrease the capacity of the cardiovascular system by constriction of the peripheral vessels in response to the heart's inability to pump sufficient blood. Veins tend to follow a course parallel to that of arteries but are present in greater number. Their

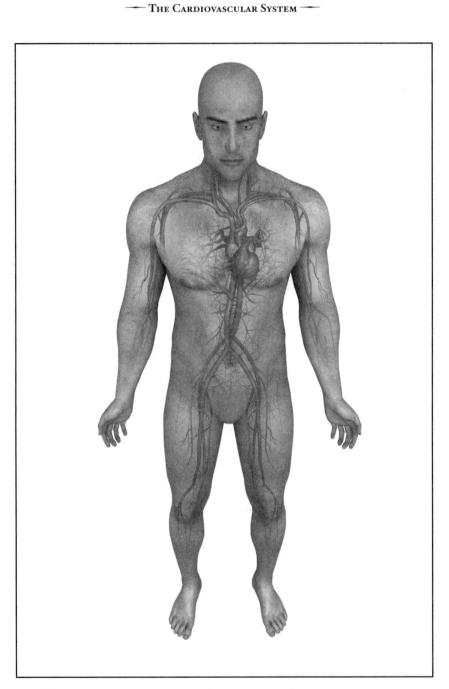

This diagram shows the human heart and vascular system or veins and arteries. 3D4Medical.com/Getty Images

channels are larger than those of arteries, and their walls are thinner. About 60 percent of the blood volume is in the systemic circulation, and 40 percent is normally present in the veins.

Venous blood pressure is extremely low compared with that in the arterial system, and thus many veins possess special valves to keep the blood moving on its return to the heart. Valves are formed by semilunar folds in the tunica intima. They are present in pairs and serve to direct the flow of blood to the heart, particularly in an upward direction. As blood flows toward the heart, the flaps of the valves flatten against the wall of the vein. They then billow out to block the opening as the pressure of the blood and surrounding tissues fills the valve pocket. These valves are more abundant in the veins of the extremities than in any other parts of the body.

VENAE CAVAE

The two venae cavae, the superior and inferior trunks, deliver oxygen-depleted blood to the right side of the heart. In mammals other than humans, the superior vena cava is known as the anterior vena cava, or the precava, and serves to drain the head end of the body, while the inferior vena cava is known as the posterior vena cava, or postcava, and drains the tail, or rear, end. Whereas many mammals, including humans, have only one anterior (or superior) vena cava, other animals have two.

Superior Vena Cava and Its Tributaries

Tributaries from the head and neck, the arms, and part of the chest unite to form the superior vena cava. In the head, venous drainage is effected by communicating vessels and by channels called venous sinuses, which lie between the two layers of the dura mater (the outer covering of the brain) and do not possess valves. The internal jugular vein is a continuation of this system downward through the neck. It receives blood from parts of the face, neck, and brain. The external jugular vein, which is formed by the union of its tributaries near the angle of the lower jaw, or mandible, drains some of the structures of the head and neck. At approximately the level of the collarbone, the subclavian, external jugular, and internal jugular veins all converge to form the innominate vein (or brachiocephalic vein). The right and left innominate veins terminate in the superior vena cava, which extends down about 7 cm (2.7 inches) before it opens into the right atrium of the heart. There is no valve at the heart opening.

In addition to the innominate veins, the superior vena cava receives blood from the azygous vein and small veins from the mediastinum (the region between the two lungs) and the pericardium. Most of the blood from the back and from the walls of the chest and abdomen drains into veins lying alongside the vertebral bodies (the weight-bearing portions of the vertebrae). These veins form what is known as the azygous system, which serves as a connecting link between the superior and inferior vena cava. The terminal veins of this system are the azygous, hemiazygous, and accessory hemiazygous veins. At the level of the diaphragm, the right ascending lumbar vein continues upward as the azygous vein, principal tributaries of which are the right intercostal veins, which drain the muscles of the intercostal spaces. It also receives tributaries from the esophagus, lymph nodes, pericardium, and right lung, and it enters into the superior vena cava at about the level of the fourth thoracic vertebra.

The left side of the azygous system varies greatly among individuals. Usually the hemiazygous vein arises just below the diaphragm as a continuation of the left ascending lumbar vein and terminates in the azygous vein. Tributaries of the hemiazygous drain the intercostal muscles, the esophagus, and a portion of the mediastinum. The accessory hemiazygous usually extends downward as a continuation of the vein of the fourth intercostal space, receiving tributaries from the left intercostal spaces and the left bronchus. It empties into the azygous vein slightly above the entrance of the hemiazygous.

All of the veins of the arm are tributaries of the subclavian veins. They are found in both superficial and deep locations and possess valves. Most of the deep veins are arranged in pairs with cross connections between them. Venous drainage of the hand is accomplished superficially by small anastomosing (inte   veins that unite to form the cephalic vein, c   ) side of the forearm, and the   ar side of the forearm and r   d, forearm, and arm. The de   de the radial veins, contin   ng veins of the hand and wris   ins following the course of the associated   dial and ulnar veins converge at the elbow to form the brachial vein. This, in turn, unites with the basilic vein at the level of the shoulder to produce the axillary vein. At the outer border of the first rib, the axillary vein becomes the subclavian vein, the terminal point of the venous system characteristic of the upper extremity.

Inferior Vena Cava and Its Tributaries

The inferior vena cava is a large, valveless, venous trunk that is formed by the coming together of the two major veins from the legs, the common iliac veins, at the level of the fifth lumbar vertebra, just below the small of the back.

Unlike the superior vena cava, it has a substantial number of tributaries between its point of origin and its terminus at the heart. These include the veins that collect blood from the muscles and coverings of the loins and from the walls of the abdomen, from the reproductive organs, from the kidneys, and from the liver. In its course to the heart, the inferior vena cava ascends close to the backbone. It passes the liver, in the dorsal surface of which it forms a groove; enters the chest through an opening in the diaphragm; and empties into the right atrium of the heart at a non-valve opening below the point of entry for the superior vena cava.

Most blood from the lower extremity returns by way of the deep veins. These include the femoral and popliteal veins and the veins accompanying the anterior and posterior tibial and peroneal arteries. The anterior and posterior tibial veins originate in the foot and join at the level of the knee to form the popliteal vein. The latter becomes the femoral vein as it continues its extension through the thigh.

The foot is drained primarily by the dorsal venous arch, which crosses the top of the foot not far from the base of the toes. The arch is connected with veins that drain the sole. Superficially the lower leg is drained by the large and small saphenous veins, which are continuations of the dorsal venous arch. The small saphenous vein extends up the back of the lower leg to terminate usually in the popliteal vein. There is some interconnection with deep veins and with the great saphenous vein. The latter vein, the longest in the body, extends from the dorsal venous arch up the inside of the lower leg and thigh, receiving venous branches from the knee and thigh area and terminating in the femoral vein.

At the level of the inguinal ligament (which is at the anterior, diagonal border between the trunk and the thigh), the femoral vein becomes known as the external iliac vein. The latter unites with the internal iliac vein to form the common iliac vein. The internal iliac vein drains the pelvic walls, viscera, external genitalia, buttocks, and a portion of the thigh. Through the paired common iliac veins, the legs and most of the pelvis are drained. The two common iliacs then unite at a level above the coccyx (the lowest bone in the spine) to become the inferior vena cava. As it courses upward through the abdomen, the inferior vena cava receives blood from the common iliacs and from the lumbar, renal, suprarenal, and hepatic veins before emptying into the right atrium. The pairs of lumbar veins (which drain blood from the loins and abdominal walls) are united on each side by a vertical connecting vein, the ascending lumbar vein. The right ascending lumbar vein continues as the azygous and the left as the hemiazygous. These veins usually enter separately into the inferior vena cava.

Renal veins lie in front of the corresponding renal artery. The right renal vein receives tributaries exclusively from the kidney, while the left receives blood from a number of other organs as well. The right suprarenal vein terminates directly in the inferior vena cava as does the right phrenic, above the gonadal vein. Two or three short hepatic trunks empty into the inferior vena cava as it passes through the diaphragm.

PORTAL SYSTEM

The portal system may be described as a specialized portion of the systemic circulatory system. Although it originates in capillaries, the portal system is unique from other vessels in that it also terminates in a capillary-like vascular bed, located in the liver. The blood from the spleen, stomach, pancreas, and intestine first passes through the liver before it moves on to the heart. Blood flowing to the liver comes from the hepatic artery (20 percent) and the portal vein (80 percent). Blood leaving the liver flows through the hepatic vein and then empties into the inferior vena cava. The hepatic arterial blood supplies oxygen requirements for the liver. Blood from the abdominal viscera, particularly the intestinal tract, passes into the portal vein and then into the liver. Substances in the portal blood are processed by the liver.

Portal Vein

The portal vein is a large vessel through which oxygen-depleted blood from the stomach, the intestines, the spleen, the gallbladder, and the pancreas flows to the liver. The principal tributaries to the portal vein are the lienal vein, with blood from the stomach, the greater omentum (a curtain of membrane and fat that hangs down over the intestines), the pancreas, the large intestine, and the spleen; the superior mesenteric vein, with blood from the small intestine and part of the large intestine; the pyloric veins, with blood from the stomach; and the cystic veins, with blood from the gallbladder. In the liver the blood from the portal vein flows through a network of microscopic vessels called sinusoids in which the blood is relieved of worn-out red cells, bacteria, and other debris and in which nutrients are added to the blood or removed from it for storage. The blood leaves the liver by way of the hepatic veins.

Hepatic Vein

The hepatic veins are vessels that transport blood from the liver to the inferior vena cava, which carries the blood to the right atrium of the heart. In its ascent to the heart, the inferior vena cava passes along a groove in the posterior side of the liver, and it is there that the hepatic veins join it. The blood transported by the hepatic veins comes not only from the liver itself but also from most of the abdominal organs. This blood flows to the liver by way of the portal vein.

VENOUS PULMONARY SYSTEM

From the pulmonary capillaries, in which blood takes on oxygen and gives up carbon dioxide, the oxygenated blood in veins is collected first into venules and then into progressively larger veins. It finally flows through four pulmonary veins, two from the hilum of each lung. (The hilum is the point of entry on each lung for the bronchus, blood vessels, and nerves.) These veins then pass to the left atrium, where their contents are poured into the heart.

CAPILLARIES

The vast network of some 10 billion microscopic capillaries functions to provide a method whereby fluids, nutrients, and wastes are exchanged between the blood and the tissues. Even though microscopic in size, the largest capillary being approximately 0.2 mm (.01 in) in diameter (about the width of the tip of a pin), the great network of capillaries serves as a reservoir normally containing about one-sixth of the total circulating blood volume. The number of capillaries in active tissue, such as muscle, liver, kidney, and lungs, is greater than the number in tendon or ligament. In addition, the cornea of the eye, epidermis, and hyaline cartilage (semitransparent cartilage such as is found in joints) are devoid of capillaries.

The interconnecting network of capillaries into which the arterioles empty is characterized not only by microscopic size but also by extremely thin walls only one cell thick. The vessels are simply tubular continuations of the inner lining cells of the larger vessels, normally uniform in size, usually three to four endothelial cells in circumference, except toward the venous terminations, where they become slightly wider, four to six cells in circumference. A thin membrane, called a basement membrane, surrounds these cells and serves to maintain the integrity of the vessel.

A single capillary unit consists of a branching and interconnecting (anastomosing) network of vessels, each averaging 0.5 to 1 mm (about 0.02 to 0.04 inch) in length. The wall of the capillary is extremely thin and acts as a semipermeable membrane that allows substances containing small molecules, such as oxygen, carbon dioxide, water, fatty acids, glucose, and ketones, to pass through the membrane. Oxygen and nutritive material pass into the tissues through the wall at the arteriolar end of the capillary unit. Carbon dioxide and waste products move through the membrane into the vessel at the venous end of the capillary bed. Constriction and dilation of the arterioles is primarily responsible for regulating the flow of blood into the capillaries. Muscular gatekeepers, or sphincters, in the capillary unit itself, however, serve to direct the flow to those areas in greatest need.

There are three modes of transport across the cellular membrane of the capillary wall. Substances soluble in the lipid (fatty) membrane of the capillary cells can pass directly through these membranes by a process of diffusion. Some substances needed by the tissues and soluble in water but completely insoluble in the lipid membrane pass through minute water-filled passageways, or pores, in the membranes by a process called ultrafiltration. Only $\frac{1}{1,000}$th of the surface area of capillaries is represented by these pores. Other substances, such as cholesterol, are transported by specific receptors in the endothelium.

PULMONARY CIRCULATION

The pulmonary circulation consists of a system of blood vessels that forms a closed circuit between the heart and the lungs, as distinguished from the systemic circulation between the heart and all other body tissues. On the evolutionary cycle, pulmonary circulation first occurs in lungfishes and amphibians, the first animals to acquire a three-chambered heart. The pulmonary circulation becomes totally separate in crocodilians, birds, and mammals, when the ventricle is divided into two chambers, producing a

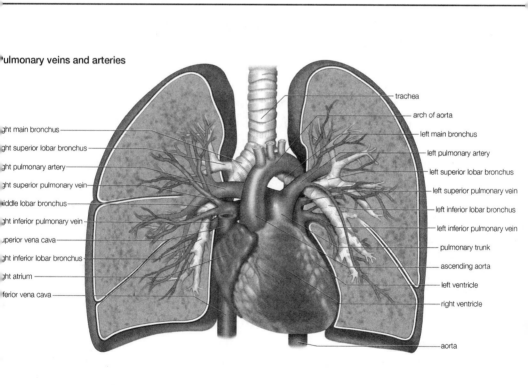

Pulmonary veins and arteries

- trachea
- arch of aorta
- left main bronchus
- left pulmonary artery
- left superior lobar bronchus
- left superior pulmonary vein
- left inferior lobar bronchus
- left inferior pulmonary vein
- pulmonary trunk
- ascending aorta
- left ventricle
- right ventricle
- aorta

right main bronchus
right superior lobar bronchus
right pulmonary artery
right superior pulmonary vein
middle lobar bronchus
right inferior pulmonary vein
superior vena cava
right inferior lobar bronchus
right atrium
inferior vena cava

The pulmonary veins and arteries in the human. Encyclopædia Britannica, Inc.

four-chambered heart. In these forms, the pulmonary circuit begins with the right ventricle, which pumps deoxygenated blood through the pulmonary artery. This artery divides above the heart into two branches, to the right and left lungs, where the arteries further subdivide into smaller and smaller branches until the capillaries in the pulmonary air sacs (alveoli) are reached. In the capillaries the blood takes up oxygen from the air breathed into the air sacs and releases carbon dioxide. It then flows into larger and larger vessels until the pulmonary veins (usually four in number, each serving a whole lobe of the lung) are reached. The pulmonary veins open into the left atrium of the heart.

The pulmonary circuit consists of the right ventricle; the exiting pulmonary artery and its branches; the arterioles, capillaries, and venules of the lungs; and the pulmonary veins that empty into the left atrium. The pulmonary trunk, the common stem of the pulmonary arteries, arises from the upper surface of the right ventricle and extends 4 to 5 cm (about 1.6 to 2.0 inches) beyond this origin before dividing into the right and left pulmonary arteries, which supply the lungs. The pulmonary valve, which has two leaflets, or cusps, guards the opening between the right ventricle and the pulmonary trunk. The trunk is relatively thin-walled for an artery, having walls approximately twice the thickness of the vena cava and one-third that of the aorta. The right and left pulmonary arteries are short but possess a relatively large diameter. The walls are distensible, allowing the vessels to accommodate the stroke volume of the right ventricle, which is a necessary function equal to that of the left ventricle.

The pulmonary trunk passes diagonally upward to the left across the route of the aorta. Between the fifth and sixth thoracic vertebrae (at about the level of the bottom of the breastbone), the trunk divides into two branches—the right and left pulmonary arteries—which, as noted, enter the lungs. After entering the lungs, the branches go through a process of subdivision, the final branches being capillaries. Capillaries surrounding the air sacs (alveoli) of the lungs pick up oxygen and release carbon dioxide. The capillaries carrying oxygenated blood join larger and larger vessels until they reach the pulmonary veins, which carry oxygenated blood from the lungs to the left atrium of the heart.

SYSTEMIC CIRCULATION

The systemic circulation consists of a circuit of vessels that supplies oxygenated blood to and returns deoxygenated blood from the tissues of the body, as distinguished from the pulmonary circulation. Blood is pumped from the left ventricle of the heart through the aorta and arterial branches to the arterioles and through capillaries, where it reaches an equilibrium with the tissue fluid, and then drains through the venules into the veins and returns, via the venae cavae, to the right atrium of the heart. Pressure in the arterial system, resulting from heart action and distension by the blood, maintains systemic blood flow. The systemic pathway, however, consists of many circuits in parallel, each of which has its own arteriolar resistance that determines blood flow independently of the overall flow and pressure and without necessarily disrupting these. For example, the blood flow through the digestive tract increases after meals, and that through working muscles increases during exercise.

HUMAN FETAL CIRCULATION

In the fetus, oxygenated blood is carried from the placenta to the fetus by the umbilical vein. It then passes to the inferior vena cava of the fetus by way of a vessel called the ductus venosus. From the inferior vena cava, the blood enters the right atrium, then passes through the foramen ovale into the left atrium. From there it moves into the left ventricle and out through the aorta, which pumps the oxygenated blood to the head and upper extremities. Blood from the upper extremities returns via the superior vena cava into the right atrium, where it is largely deflected into the right ventricle.

From the right ventricle, a portion of the blood flows into the pulmonary artery to the lungs. The largest fraction flows through an opening, the ductus arteriosus, into the aorta. It enters the aorta beyond the point at which the blood of the head leaves. Some of the blood supplies the lower portion of the body. The remainder returns to the placenta via the umbilical arteries, which branch off from the internal iliac arteries.

ANGIOGENESIS

Angiogenesis is the formation of new blood vessels. It is a normal process during growth of the body and in the body's replacement of damaged tissue. However, it can also occur under abnormal conditions, such as in tumour progression. At some point, after months or even years as a harmless cluster of cells, tumours may suddenly begin to generate blood vessels — apparently because they develop the ability to synthesize certain growth factors that stimulate the formation of vessels.

Angiogenesis is an important step that a tumour undergoes in its transition to life-threatening malignancy (cancer). When tumour cells reach this transition, they call on proteins that stimulate capillary growth and develop the ability themselves to synthesize proteins with this capacity. One of these proteins is known as vascular endothelial growth factor (VEGF). VEGF induces endothelial cells (the building blocks of capillaries) to penetrate a tumour nodule and begin the process of capillary development. As the endothelial cells divide, they in turn secrete growth factors that stimulate the growth or motility of tumour cells. Thus, endothelial cells and tumour cells mutually stimulate each other.

Cancer cells also produce another type of protein that inhibits the growth of blood vessels. Evidence suggests that angiogenesis begins when cells decrease their production of the inhibiting proteins. Angiogenesis inhibitors are seen as promising therapeutic agents.

CHAPTER 3
CONGENITAL HEART DISEASE

Modern knowledge of how the various components of the cardiovascular system function and interact has come largely from the study, diagnosis, and treatment of cardiovascular diseases and disorders. Careful investigation into why and how cardiovascular dysfunction occurs also has led scientists to the discovery of certain biochemical processes and genetic factors that underlie the health and normal functioning of the cardiovascular system. Thus, a general understanding of cardiovascular anatomy and function is enhanced significantly by explorations into the diverse array of known cardiovascular pathologies.

In the 20th century, the discovery and study of conditions known as congenital heart diseases, which are abnormalities of the heart that are present at birth, served to tremendously advance scientists' knowledge of the embryological development of the heart and heart anatomy in neonates as well as adults. Although most cardiac defects are caused by abnormal development of the heart and circulatory system before birth, certain types of defects may not be diagnosed until much later in life and, in some cases, may not be diagnosed at all.

Abnormal heart development can be caused by a variety of factors, including infection and use of certain drugs by the mother during pregnancy. Some congenital cardiac abnormalities are inherited and may be transmitted as sex-linked traits, in which causative mutations occur on the X or Y chromosomes, or as autosomal traits, in which causative mutations occur on any of the other 22 chromosomes. However, for some of the more common abnormalities, there is no obvious heritable relationship, nor is the origin of the disease readily explained.

The heart's complicated evolution during embryological development presents the opportunity for many different types of congenital defects to occur. Thus, congenital cardiac disturbances are varied and may involve almost all components of the heart and great arteries. Some may cause death at the time of birth, others may not have an effect until early adulthood, and some may be associated with an essentially normal life span.

Nonetheless, about 40 percent of all untreated infants born with congenital heart disease die before the end of their first year, and some congenital cardiac defects in particular are associated with high neonatal and infant mortality. One example is hypoplastic left heart syndrome, a very serious condition in which the left ventricle and other structures are underdeveloped, severely compromising blood flow through the body. Fortunately, surgical advances have made it possible to correct many defects, so that some patients who once would have succumbed at a very young age now lead longer and relatively normal lives. For some congenital heart disease patients, a heart transplant or combined heart-lung transplant is an option.

CAUSES AND DIAGNOSIS OF CONGENITAL HEART DISEASE

Congenital heart disease is one of the important types of diseases affecting the cardiovascular system, with an incidence of about 8 per 1,000 live births. In most patients the causes appear to fit in the middle of a continuum from primarily genetic to primarily environmental.

Of the few cases that have a genetic nature, the defect may be the result of a single mutant gene, while in other cases it may be associated with a chromosomal abnormality, the most common of which is Down syndrome, in which about 50 percent of afflicted children have a congenital cardiac abnormality. In the even smaller number of cases of an obvious environmental cause, a variety of specific factors are evident. The occurrence of rubella (German measles) in a woman during the first three months of pregnancy is caused by a virus and is associated in the child with patent ductus arteriosus (nonclosure of the opening between the aorta and the pulmonary artery). Other viruses may be responsible for specific heart lesions, and a number of drugs, including antiepileptic agents, are associated with an increased incidence of congenital heart disease.

In most cases, congenital heart disease is probably caused by a variety of factors, and any genetic factor is usually unmasked only if it occurs together with the appropriate environmental hazard. The risk of a sibling of a child with congenital heart disease being similarly affected is between 2 and 4 percent. The precise recurrence can vary for individual congenital cardiovascular lesions.

Prenatal diagnosis of congenital cardiovascular abnormalities is still at an early stage. The most promising technique is ultrasonography, used for many years to examine the fetus in utero. The increasing sophistication of equipment has made it possible to examine the heart and the great vessels from 16 to 18 weeks of gestation onward and to determine whether defects are present. Amniocentesis (removal and examination of a small quantity of fluid from around the developing fetus) provides a method by which the fetal chromosomes can be examined for chromosomal abnormalities associated with congenital heart disease. In many children and adults the presence of congenital heart disease is detected for the first time when a cardiac murmur is heard. A congenital cardiovascular lesion is rarely signaled by a disturbance of the heart rate or the heart rhythm.

TYPES OF CONGENITAL HEART DISEASES

Congenital abnormalities are distinguished by the type of defect present. One of the most common abnormalities is a simple septal defect, where a hole is found in the partition, or septum, between the right atrium and left atrium or between the right ventricle and left ventricle of the heart.

Another type of congenital abnormality affects the heart valves, causing valvular insufficiency or obstruction. As with septal defects, valve defects generally can be repaired by surgery. More complicated defects, however, often involve a combination of abnormalities. An example can be seen in tetralogy of Fallot, a condition where there is narrowing of the valve to the pulmonary artery (pulmonary stenosis), a ventricular septal defect, an aorta that overrides both the right and left ventricle so that it receives blood from both sides of the heart, and severe thickening of the muscle of the right ventricle (right ventricular hypertrophy). As a result of these defects, the circulating blood is deprived of oxygen, causing the bluish discoloration of the skin known as blue baby syndrome.

Yet another group of congenital heart defects affects the aorta and the pulmonary artery. In the complex abnormality known as transposition of the great arteries, the aorta rises from the right ventricle, which under normal anatomic configurations pumps blood to the lungs. At the same time, the pulmonary artery, the conduit of blood to the lungs, rises from the left ventricle, which normally pumps blood through the aorta to the body.

Another condition is patent ductus arteriosus, where a temporary channel that connects the pulmonary artery and the first segment of the descending thoracic aorta during fetal growth fails to close after birth, causing some mixing of oxygenated and deoxygenated blood. In coarctation of the aorta, another type of defect, the aorta may be narrowed just below the point where the arteries supplying the upper part of the body emerge, thus increasing blood pressure in the upper half of the body and reducing pressure in the lower half of the body.

Depending on the constellation of abnormalities, congenital heart disease is often categorized as either cyanotic (causing a bluish skin colour) or noncyanotic. Cyanosis occurs when a mixture of oxygenated and deoxygenated blood courses through the arteries. The condition arises from the presence of a shunt that bypasses the lungs and delivers venous (deoxygenated) blood from the right side of the heart into the arterial circulation. This brings on the blue-red-violet hue characteristic of the excess deoxygenated blood in the system. Thus, cyanosis typically manifests as a change in colour in the infant's nail beds and lips, which typically have a blue tint. Some infants with severe noncyanotic varieties of congenital heart disease may fail to thrive and may have breathing difficulties.

ABNORMALITIES OF INDIVIDUAL HEART CHAMBERS

Abnormalities of the heart chambers may be serious and even life-threatening. In hypoplastic left heart syndrome, the left-sided heart chambers, including the aorta, are underdeveloped. Infants born with this condition rarely survive more than two or three days. In other cases, only one chamber develops adequately. Survival often depends on the presence of associated compensatory abnormalities, such as continued patency of the ductus arteriosus or the presence of a septal defect, which may allow either decompression of a chamber under elevated pressure or beneficial compensatory intracardiac shunting either from right to left or from left to right.

ABNORMALITIES OF THE ATRIAL SEPTUM

A congenital opening in the partition between the two atria of the heart is known as an atrial septal defect. The presence of an atrial defect allows blood to be shunted from the left side of the heart to the right, with an increase in blood flow and volume within the pulmonary circulation. Thus, an atrial septal defect causes a sort of short circuit to develop where more blood flows through the lungs than through the other organs of the body. In addition, the hole between the two sides of the heart produces an abnormal mixture of oxygenated blood from the pulmonary circulation and deoxygenated blood from the systemic circulation.

Defects in the atrial septum may be small or large and occur most commonly in the midportion in the area prenatally occupied by the aperture called the foramen ovale (the opening of the foramen ovale is normal before birth and normally closes at birth or shortly thereafter). The persistence of the foramen ovale in the atrial septum results in the flow of blood from the left atrium to the right, causing enlargement of the right atrium and ventricle and of the main pulmonary artery. Defects lower on the atrial septum may involve the atrioventricular valves and may be associated with incompetence of these valves. In its most extreme form, there may be virtually no septum between the two atrial chambers.

A small atrial defect may be associated with problems in young adults, although deterioration can occur in later life. Over many years the added burden on the right side of the heart and the elevation of the blood pressure in the lungs may severely compromise the heart. Indeed, septal defects ultimately may cause thickening of the walls of the pulmonary artery as well as pulmonary hypertension (high blood pressure). Increased stress may be placed on the right ventricle as it tries to pump blood through the pulmonary circuits for oxygenation. Right heart failure may then develop, and the supply of appropriately oxygenated blood to the body tissues may become compromised.

Atrial septal defect is a noncyanotic type of congenital heart disease and usually is not associated with serious disability during childhood. However, atrial septal defects, unless small, must usually be closed in childhood. Defects of the atrium and ventricle can be repaired surgically with ease and great success as long as severe, irreversible pulmonary hypertension has not developed.

ABNORMALITIES OF THE VENTRICULAR SEPTUM

Defects in the interventricular septum, the partition that separates the lower chambers of the heart, may be small or large, single or multiple, and may exist within any part of the ventricular septum. Small defects are among the most common congenital cardiovascular abnormalities and may be less life-threatening, since many such defects close spontaneously. Small defects often create loud murmurs but, because there is limited flow of blood from left to right, no significant change in the circulation occurs. On the other hand, when a defect is large, a significant amount of blood is shunted from the left ventricle to the right, with a high flow and volume of blood into the pulmonary circulation.

The pulmonary circulation may be damaged by the stresses imposed by a high blood flow over a long period of time. If unchecked, this damage can become irreversible. A further hazard in both small and large ventricular septal defects is the increased risk of bacterial endocarditis (inflammation of the heart lining as a result of bacterial infection). This risk is likely to be high during procedures such as dental extractions, when infection may enter the bloodstream.

Ventricular septal defects are often combined with other congenital cardiac defects. The best-known of these is tetralogy of Fallot.

Tetralogy of Fallot

Tetralogy of Fallot, also called Fallot tetrad, is a combination of congenital heart defects characterized by hypoxic spells (which include difficulty in breathing and alterations in consciousness), a change in the shape of the fingertips (digital clubbing), heart murmur, and cyanosis, which causes the bluish discoloration of the skin that gives rise to the consequent blue baby syndrome. Named for French physician Étienne-Louis-Arthur Fallot, who first described it in the late 19th century, tetralogy of Fallot, as mentioned above, is the result of a combination of a defect in the ventricular septum, pulmonary stenosis (narrowing of the opening to the pulmonary artery), dilation and displacement of the aorta to override the ventricular septum, and right ventricular hypertrophy (thickening of the muscle of the right ventricle). As a result of the obstruction imposed by the pulmonary stenosis, deoxygenated venous blood is shunted from the right to the left side of the heart into the arterial circulation.

Significant amounts of deoxygenated blood in the systemic circulation impart a cyanotic, blue-gray cast to the skin. A child with this cyanotic form of congenital heart disease can survive beyond infancy, but few survive to adulthood without surgery. Total correction of the condition is possible with surgical repair of the septal defect, removal of the obstruction to the right ventricular outflow, and opening of the right ventricle.

Pulmonary Stenosis

Pulmonary stenosis, as noted in the discussion of tetralogy of Fallot, is the narrowing of either the pulmonary valve—the valve through which blood flows from the right ventricle of the heart on its way to the lungs—or the infundibulum, or of both. The infundibulum (Latin: "funnel") is the funnel-shaped portion of the right ventricle that opens into the pulmonary artery. Its narrowing is also called infundibular stenosis. Pulmonary stenosis is usually a congenital defect and may be associated with other cardiovascular congenital defects.

Persons may have mild pulmonary stenosis without being conscious of the defect or may experience difficulty in breathing and have a tendency to faint after exertion. Characteristic heart sounds lead to the diagnosis.

If the stenosis is severe, the right ventricle is enlarged and under abnormal pressure in the effort to maintain normal blood flow to the lungs. Failure to maintain adequate blood flow—right-sided heart failure—causes increased pressure in the peripheral veins, enlargement of the liver, cyanosis, and accumulation of fluid in the legs. The treatment for severe pulmonary stenosis is the surgical correction of the defect.

ABNORMAL ORIGINS OF THE GREAT ARTERIES

In many complex forms of congenital heart disease, the aorta and pulmonary artery do not originate from their normal areas of the ventricles. In one of the most common of such cases—transposition of the great arteries—the aorta originates from the right ventricle and receives deoxygenated blood from the superior and inferior venae cavae, and the pulmonary artery arises from the left ventricle and receives fully oxygenated pulmonary venous blood. Survival in such cases depends on a naturally occurring communication between the two sides of the heart that allows oxygenated blood to enter the aorta. If such a communication is not present naturally, it may be created medically or surgically. Both the aorta and the pulmonary artery may originate from the right ventricle. This form of abnormal origin of the arteries usually is associated with a ventricular septal defect and, on occasion, pulmonary stenosis. This combination of defects is a severe form of cyanotic heart disease.

ABNORMALITIES OF THE VALVES

The most common congenital abnormality of the cardiac valves affects the aortic valve. The normal aortic valve usually has three cusps, or leaflets, but the valve is bicuspid in 1 to 2 percent of the population. A bicuspid aortic valve is not necessarily life-threatening, but in some persons it becomes thickened and obstructed (stenotic). With age the valve may also become incompetent or act as a nidus (focus of infection) for bacterial endocarditis. Congenital aortic valve stenosis, if severe, results in hypertrophy of the left ventricular myocardium and may rarely be responsible for sudden death in asymptomatic individuals. Even minor forms of aortic valve stenosis may grow progressively severe and are likely, with the passage of time, to require surgical treatment.

In contrast to aortic valve stenosis, pulmonary valve stenosis, if mild, is usually well tolerated and does not require surgical treatment. More severe forms of the disease may require surgery or balloon dilation.

ABNORMALITIES OF THE MYOCARDIUM
AND ENDOCARDIUM

Congenital abnormalities in the myocardium—for example, tumours—may be present at birth, but they are rare. Abnormalities of the endocardium may be present at birth, but they are also rare. They include fibroelastosis, a disease in which the endocardium develops a thick fibrous coat that interferes with the normal contraction and relaxation of the heart. This condition cannot be treated surgically and is usually life-threatening.

ABNORMALITIES OF THE CORONARY ARTERIES

The coronary arteries may arise abnormally from a pulmonary artery rather than from the aorta, with the result that deoxygenated blood instead of oxygenated blood flows through the heart muscle. Abnormal openings, called coronary arterial venous fistulas, may be present between the coronary arteries and the chambers of the heart. One or more of the three main coronary arteries may be absent. While these abnormalities are frequently asymptomatic, they may be associated with early, often sudden, death. If necessary, most coronary arterial abnormalities can be corrected surgically.

ABNORMALITIES OF THE AORTA

One of the most common congenital cardiovascular abnormalities involves the aorta. Coarctation of the aorta is a congenital malformation involving the constriction, or narrowing, of a short section of that portion of the aorta that arches over the heart. The narrowing of the aortic wall usually occurs at that portion of the aorta just beyond the site at which the main blood vessel to the left arm (the subclavian artery) originates.

As a result of the narrowing or obstruction at this point, blood flow to the lower half of the body—the abdomen, pelvis, and legs—is diminished, and hypertension develops in the upper half of the body. In addition, the partial obstruction of the aortic channel causes a characteristic murmur, and the left ventricle is usually enlarged. Intercostal (between-the-ribs) branches from the aorta enlarge and cause characteristic notching of the ribs. Coarctation of the aorta may give rise to heart failure in early infancy or complications in later childhood and adulthood.

Patent ductus arteriosus is another congenital heart defect involving the aorta. It is characterized by the persistence of the ductus arteriosus, a channel that shunts blood between the pulmonary artery and the aorta. During fetal life and immediately following birth, the ductus arteriosus connects the pulmonary artery and the first segment of the descending thoracic aorta. The function of this duct in utero is to shunt blood away from the lungs. Consequently, most of the blood pumped into the pulmonary artery is sent through the ductus arteriosus into the aorta for distribution into the general circulation. Normally, at birth the ductus arteriosus constricts and closes, becoming a fibromuscular cord. However, if the ductus remains open after birth, excessive blood may flow into the lungs, resulting in pulmonary congestion and heart failure.

Spontaneous closure of the ductus arteriosus may be delayed in premature newborn infants, exacerbating the respiratory problems common to them. If necessary, the ductus arteriosus can be induced to close with drugs in premature infants, and it can be closed in older infants and children by surgery or insertion of a prosthetic occluder by cardiac catheterization. Finally, there may be direct communication between the aorta and pulmonary arteries because the truncus arteriosus has either partially or completely failed to partition.

If the passageway is large, it can have serious effects, acting as a shunt that carries blood from the aorta into the pulmonary artery. This reversal of the shunt pathway occurs because, as a normal part of the changes from fetal

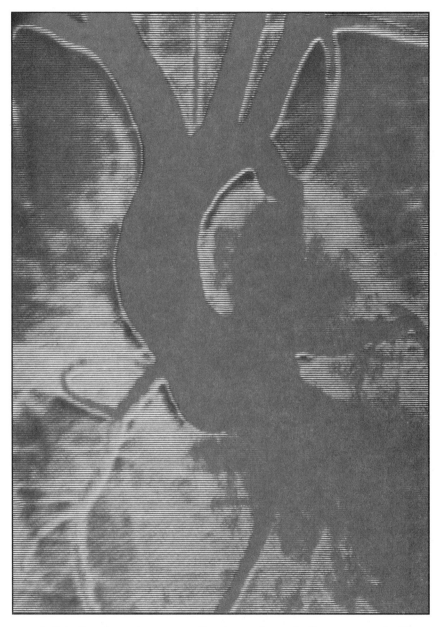

A digitally enhanced aortogram (aortic arteriogram) of a seven-month-old infant in which two congenital abnormalities, patent ductus arteriosus and an atrial septal defect, are visible. Cardiothoracic Centre, Freeman Hospital, Newcastle upon Tyne/Photo Researchers, Inc.

to postnatal circulation, the blood pressure in the aorta rises greatly, while that in the pulmonary artery falls. As a consequence of this shunt, the blood may be routed two or three times from the left ventricle to the lungs before it follows its normal course into the systemic circulation. The left side of the heart is thus greatly overworked and becomes enlarged, and the lungs become congested and their network of blood vessels becomes damaged from excessive blood pressure. As a result, the body is deprived of adequate oxygen during exertion—or, in extreme cases, even during rest. The oxygen deprivation is indicated by cyanosis.

ANOMALOUS PULMONARY VENOUS RETURN

The pulmonary veins from the right and left lungs may connect either directly or indirectly to the right, instead of the left, atrium. In this condition the abnormal venous channel draining to the right side of the heart may become obstructed. Infants born with total anomalous (abnormal) pulmonary venous drainage usually develop problems within the first few weeks or months and thus require cardiac surgery. Partial forms of anomalous pulmonary venous return, in which only one or two pulmonary veins are connected abnormally, may have few symptoms, although surgical correction may be done if required.

ANOMALIES OF THE VENAE CAVAE

The most common abnormalities of the venae cavae, the major veins returning venous blood to the right side of the heart, are a persistent left superior vena cava (normally there is only one superior vena cava opening to the right side of the heart) and an abnormal connection of the inferior vena cava to the heart. These abnormalities are frequently associated with intracardiac structural faults.

REPAIR OF CONGENITAL CARDIAC DEFECTS

Most congenital cardiac defects can be repaired surgically. Operations are of two general types: those that can be performed without a heart-lung machine, such as surgeries for patent ductus arteriosus and coarctation of the aorta, and those, such as intracardiac abnormalities, that require a heart-lung machine.

If atrial and ventricular septal defects require surgical closure, the patient's circulation must be supported by the heart-lung machine. Atrial septal defects are usually repaired by sewing the tissue on either side of the defect together, although very large defects may require a patch of material to close the opening. Because of the frequency of spontaneous natural closure, small ventricular septal defects are observed for a period of time before the decision is made to perform surgery. Large ventricular septal defects are usually closed by a patch.

The most common congenital defect of the valves in children is pulmonary stenosis (see "Pulmonary stenosis" section on page 77). The valve cusps in this condition are not well formed, and, as a result, the valve cannot open normally. Mild stenosis is usually compatible with normal activities and normal life, but moderate and severe stenosis may result in clear symptoms.

The surgical procedure used to correct this condition is usually performed on cardiopulmonary bypass, with the valve approached through the pulmonary artery and cut in three places to create a valve with three cusps. An alternative approach to surgery is the use of a special balloon catheter, which is passed from the femoral vein (the vein in the groin) into the right side of the heart and positioned across the pulmonary valve. A balloon at the tip of the catheter is then inflated to enlarge the valve orifice.

Although mild aortic valve stenosis is manageable in children, deterioration may occur with growth. Severe aortic stenosis in infancy and childhood may be associated with either sudden death or heart failure. The usual basis for the stenosis is fusion of the valve, which is usually bicuspid rather than tricuspid. The valve is often both obstructed and incompetent (allowing blood to leak back from the aorta into the left ventricle). Patients with more than a trivial degree of aortic stenosis usually should not take part in competitive sports, such as swimming or football. In moderate to severe degrees of aortic stenosis, surgery usually is necessary and is performed using cardiopulmonary bypass. The aorta is opened just above the valve, and the surgeon incises the valve sufficiently to convert severe stenosis to a mild or moderate degree of obstruction. In older patients the valve is often thickened and calcified, and it may need to be replaced.

The first attempt to treat "blue babies" affected with cyanotic abnormalities was performed by U.S. physicians Alfred Blalock and Helen B. Taussig in 1944. This procedure transformed the outlook for cyanotic children and for the first time made survival possible. In the early 1950s, heart-lung cardiac surgery and procedures for repair were developed. Surgical treatment of the tetralogy of Fallot has been an important model for developments in more complex forms of cardiac surgery, and long-term results have been excellent. Most, but not all, forms of cyanotic congenital heart disease can now be repaired, and palliative surgery may produce considerable benefits for those in whom definitive treatment is not possible.

Treatment of coarctation of the aorta is surgical and varies with the age of the person affected. Repair of coarctation of the aorta was first successfully performed by Clarence Crafoord in Sweden in 1944. In older children and adolescents the narrowed area is repaired by cutting out the constriction and stitching the two normal ends together. In infants a modified operation is used in which the left subclavian artery (the artery that supplies the left arm) is tied, divided, and used as a flap to repair the narrowed aortic area. With this procedure the stricture has less of a tendency to redevelop at that site. In adults it often may be necessary to bridge the narrowed area or to provide a way for blood to bypass the constricted area to reach the organs below the defect. Thus, in older persons, either the constricted section of artery is replaced with a section of tubing made from a synthetic fibre such as Dacron™, or the defect is left but is bypassed by a Dacron™ tube opening into the aorta on either side of the defect—a permanent bypass for the blood flow. Surgery for this condition is most effective in young persons and is rarely performed on patients over the age of 50.

Patent ductus arteriosus is diagnosed from characteristic abnormalities of the heart sounds. Infants with the defect can be treated with drugs that effectively close the shunt in many cases. If drug therapy is unsuccessful, the ductus can be closed by the insertion of a prosthesis by cardiac catheterization. Rarely, if the ductus arteriosus remains open, allowing excessive levels of blood to flow through the lungs, ligation may be necessary. Ligation of the ductus arteriosus performed by Robert E. Gross in Boston in 1938 was the first successful operation for congenital heart disease and initiated the modern era of cardiac surgery for congenital cardiovascular lesions.

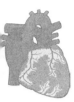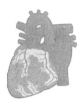

CHAPTER 4
ACQUIRED HEART DISEASE

A cquired heart diseases are conditions that are contracted during the life of an individual, as distinguished from those that are present at birth. Included in the category of acquired cardiovascular diseases are conditions such as coronary artery disease and heart attack, or myocardial infarction. These two conditions alone represent major causes of health problems and death in developed countries.

Whether or not a person develops an acquired heart disease depends on a number of factors, including age, sex, diet, physical activity, and family history of disease. Typical negative environmental influences on cardiovascular health include cigarette smoking and a diet high in sodium and fats known as low-density lipoproteins (LDLs). Such factors contribute to the deterioration of vascular function. As blood pressure increases and fats accumulate in arteries and veins, the risk of coronary heart disease, heart attack, and similar conditions increases substantially. In contrast to inherited cardiovascular diseases, over which affected individuals have very little control concerning disease onset and severity, a number of acquired heart diseases often can be prevented or managed through dietary improvements supplemented with appropriate exercise and drug regimens.

CORONARY ARTERY DISEASE

The term *coronary artery disease* describes the diseases that lead to obstruction of the flow of blood in the vessels

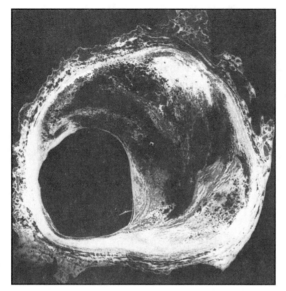

A typical atheromatous plaque in a coronary artery. The plaque has reduced the lumen (large dark circle at bottom left) to 30 percent of its normal size. The white areas are lipid and cholesterol deposits. The darker layers represent fibrous areas that have probably been scarred from earlier incorporation of thrombi from the lumen. The presence of an atheromatous plaque is a sign of atherosclerosis.

that supply the heart. These diseases can occur in other arteries as well. The term *coronary artery disease* is commonly used as a synonym for the much more specific condition of atheromatous intrusion into the artery lumen (cavity). *Coronary heart disease* is a term used to describe all of the symptoms and features that can result from advanced coronary artery disease. The same symptoms are also diagnosed as ischemic heart disease, because the symptoms result from the development of myocardial ischemia (reduced blood flow to the heart muscle). There is no one-to-one relationship between coronary atherosclerosis and the clinical symptoms of coronary artery disease or between coronary artery disease and coronary heart disease.

Coronary artery disease due to atherosclerosis is present to varying degrees in all adults in industrialized nations. The symptoms of the disease, however, will occur only when the extent of the lesions or the development of acute thrombosis (the formation of a blood clot which blocks a coronary artery) reduces the flow of blood to the heart muscle below a critical level. One or more major coronary arteries may progressively narrow without leading to any symptoms of coronary heart disease, provided the area of the heart muscle supplied by that artery is adequately supplied with blood from another coronary artery circuit. The small coronary arteries anastomose (interconnect) and are not, as previously thought, end arteries. Thus, they can open up and provide a collateral, or supportive, circulation that protects against progressive occlusion (obstruction). Exercise improves coronary collateral flow and for this reason may protect against coronary heart disease.

Although coronary artery disease is most frequently caused by atherosclerosis, inflammation of the blood vessels may, in rare cases, cause obstructive lesions of the coronary vessels. In persons with familial hypercholesterolemia (genetically inherited high cholesterol), the disease may involve the mouth of the coronary vessels as they leave the aorta and cause an obstruction to blood flow. On rare occasions, clots arising from the left atrium or left ventricle may enter the coronary vessels and cause acute obstruction and symptoms of disease.

There are influences, or "triggers," that convert coronary artery disease into coronary heart disease. These include coronary thrombosis (formation of blood clots), coronary spasm, and the hemodynamic (blood-flow) needs of the heart muscle. Influences within the heart muscle itself also may increase the demand for blood flow above the level available, making the myocardium vulnerable to alterations in function, contractility, and the maintenance of normal rhythm.

CORONARY HEART DISEASE

Coronary heart disease is a general term for a number of syndromes. Ischemic heart disease, an alternative term, is actually more correct because the syndromes described are all to some degree manifestations of myocardial ischemia (a lack of blood supply to the myocardium, or heart muscle).

Coronary heart disease includes a number of inter-dependent syndromes: angina pectoris, acute myocardial infarction (death of some tissue of the heart muscle because of reduced blood supply), and sudden cardiac death (due to lethal arrhythmia—that is, irregular heart rhythm). There are also features of coronary occlusion (blockage of a coronary artery) that indicate the presence of myocardial ischemia. Knowledge of the mechanisms that lead to a particular syndrome is inexact. Thus, a coronary thrombosis may lead to heart attack in one person, sudden death in another, a minor episode of angina in a third, or no symptoms at all in a fourth. There is, however, no alternative to using the orthodox syndromes as the means of recognizing and recording the incidence of coronary heart disease.

Epidemiology

Coronary heart disease is the leading cause of death worldwide, although its occurrence is unevenly distributed. It is the most common single cause of death in North America and Europe. The only region in which another cause of death leads heart disease is Africa. The disease was once relatively uncommon in Asia (including China, Japan, India, and the Middle East), central Africa, and Central and South America. As Western diets become more prevalent in these countries, however, the incidence of heart disease rises accordingly. Thus, although rates for heart disease were once low all over Asia and are still low in Japan, the incidence of heart disease in China is increasing steadily. Studies have linked the geographic differences in coronary heart disease with diet and with various aspects of lifestyle, such as cigarette smoking, physical inactivity, and obesity.

RISK FACTORS

Three main risk factors have been identified: cigarette smoking, a high level of cholesterol in the blood (hypercholesterolemia), and high blood pressure (hypertension). Important as these risk factors are, they are found only in about one-half of those who experience heart attacks. The proportion of persons with any or all of these three risk factors is greater in young and middle-aged adults than in older adults. It is impossible to incriminate any one of these risk factors over another, since the manifestations of coronary heart disease are undoubtedly due to many independent and interdependent influences, but the coexistence of the three greatly increases the risk of developing the disease.

The familial predisposition to the disease is not well understood, although it is stronger in families with hypercholesterolemia and hypertension. It is most likely to develop prematurely in the presence of familial (genetic) hypercholesterolemia. There is a progressive relationship between serum cholesterol concentrations and the incidence of coronary heart disease. This is also true for hypertension. Of the three major risk factors, however, excessive cigarette smoking is probably the most important. Other influences—such as a predisposition to develop thrombosis, diabetes mellitus, physical inactivity, obesity, and, rarely, oral contraceptives—may induce premature coronary heart disease in susceptible persons.

ANGINA PECTORIS

The term *angina pectoris* was first used in 1772 by the British physician William Heberden when he wrote:

There is a disorder of the breast. . . . The seat of it, and sense of strangling and anxiety, with which it is attended, may make it not improperly be called angina pectoris. Those, who are afflicted with it, are ceased [sic] while they are walking and most particularly when they walk soon after eating, with a painful and most disagreeable sensation in the breast, which seems as it would take their breath away, if it were to increase or to continue; the moment they stand still, all this uneasiness vanishes.

Heberden's initial description is still accurate. However, there are no truly characteristic symptoms of angina pectoris. Whereas the chest discomfort may be variously described as "constricting," "suffocating," "crushing," "heavy," or "squeezing," there are many patients in whom the quality of the sensation is imprecise. The discomfort is usually, but not always, behind the breastbone, but pain radiating to the throat or jaw or down the inner sides of either arm is common. There may be no physical abnormalities, and an electrocardiogram may be normal or show only transient changes with exercise.

Today, angina pectoris is described medically as a spasm of pain in the chest, usually caused by the inability of diseased coronary arteries to deliver sufficient oxygen-laden blood to the heart muscle. When insufficient blood reaches the heart, waste products accumulate in the heart muscle and irritate local nerve endings, causing a deep, viselike pain that is felt beneath the breastbone and over the heart and stomach, sometimes radiating into the left shoulder and down the inner side of the left arm. A feeling of constriction or suffocation often accompanies the pain, though there is seldom actual difficulty in breathing. Pain usually subsides after three or four minutes. In acute cases, the skin becomes pale and the pulse is weak. Anginal pain may be quite mild in some cases, but its peculiar qualities can still induce anxiety.

Attacks of angina can be precipitated by walking or more strenuous exertion, by anger, fear, or other stressful emotional states, by exercising after a large meal, or simply from exposure to cold or wind. Attacks are apt to recur following less or no exertion as coronary heart disease worsens. Angina pectoris is rare in persons under middle age and is much more common in males than in females.

Coronary arteriography assesses the extent of coronary artery occlusion (blockage), which may vary from a small increase in coronary artery muscle tone at a partly blocked site in a branch of one of the three main coronary arteries to a 90 percent or greater blockage of the left main coronary artery with involvement of other major coronary arteries. But the extent of coronary artery disease revealed by coronary arteriography does not predicate action or treatment.

The myocardial ischemia (reduced blood supply to the heart muscle) that causes angina is due to a disturbance of the balance between heart muscle demands and supply. If demands are reduced sufficiently, the temporarily endangered supply may be adequate. The disturbance of the equilibrium may be short lived and may correct itself. Unstable angina has an appreciably worse prognosis than stable angina because of a higher risk of heart attack (or myocardial infarction, meaning tissue death of a piece of the heart muscle) and sudden cardiac death, and it requires daily observation and active intervention.

In cases where the narrowing of the coronary arteries appears serious enough to cause a heart attack, methods must be used to widen the passages within the arteries or surgically replace the arteries with unblocked ones from another portion of the body. When coronary arteriography reveals relatively isolated, incompletely obstructive lesions, there are two alternative treatments— medication or coronary angioplasty (balloon dilation of the localized obstruction by a special catheter). When coronary arteriography reveals a severe blockage of the left main coronary artery or proximally in one or more of the major arteries, coronary artery bypass graft surgery may be necessary.

In unstable angina pectoris, coronary arteriography may help determine whether coronary angioplasty or coronary artery bypass surgery is needed. Drugs that cause coronary dilation and peripheral arterial vasodilation (dilation of blood vessels) and that reduce the load on the heart are usually necessary. An example of an agent that is commonly used to dilate blood vessels is nitroglycerin. Drugs that reduce the work of the heart by blocking adrenoreceptors (receptors in the heart that respond to epinephrine) and drugs that reduce a patient's tendency to form blood clots are given at this stage. For patients with stable angina, drugs that reduce the heart's work are administered. The frequency of attacks can be lessened by the avoidance of emotional stress and by shifting to exercise that is less vigorous.

HEART ATTACK

Heart attack, also called myocardial infarction, as noted above, is the death of a section of the myocardium that is caused by an interruption of blood flow to the area. A heart attack results from obstruction of the coronary arteries. The most common cause is a blood clot (thrombus) that lodges in an area of a coronary artery thickened with cholesterol-containing plaque due to atherosclerosis.

A syndrome of prolonged, severe chest pain was first described in medical literature in 1912 by James Bryan

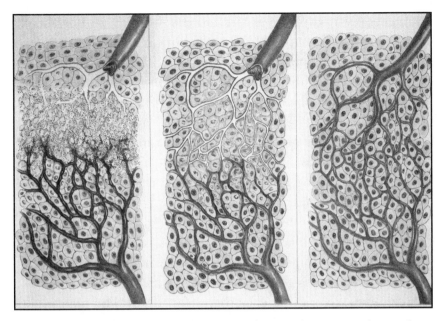

Three phases of a heart attack (myocardial infarction), beginning with normal flow of oxygenated blood (right), to the acute phase of a heart attack (middle), to infarcted (irreparably damaged) tissue (left). De Agostini Picture Library/Getty Images

Herrick, who attributed the syndrome to coronary thrombosis, the development of a clot in a major blood vessel serving the heart. As a result, the disorder was termed coronary thrombosis or coronary occlusion (blockage of a coronary artery). Later evidence indicated, however, that, though thrombotic occlusion of an atheromatous lesion in a coronary artery is the most common cause of the disorder, the manifestations are the result of the death of an area of heart muscle (infarction). The term *myocardial infarction*, therefore, is more appropriate. The less specific term *heart attack* may be more desirable because of these difficulties in describing the causation of the disease entity.

Myocardial infarction is characterized by cellular death (necrosis) of a segment of the heart muscle.

Generally, it involves an area in the forward wall of the heart related to the blood distribution of the anterior descending coronary artery, though in other instances the inferior wall or the septum (partition) of the ventricle is involved. A blocked coronary artery is present in a majority of the hearts examined at autopsy and undoubtedly plays an important role. In some instances, changes in metabolic demands of the heart muscle in the presence of a restricted blood flow may be enough to cause the death of blood-deprived cells.

The outstanding clinical feature of myocardial infarction is pain, similar in many respects to that of angina pectoris. The important difference is that the pain lasts for a much longer period—at least half an hour and usually for several hours and perhaps for days. The pain is described as "crushing," "compressing," and "like a vise" and is often associated with some difficulty in breathing. As with angina pectoris, the pain may radiate to the left arm or up the neck into the jaw. There is often nausea, vomiting, and weakness. Fainting (syncope) may occur. The affected person is frequently pale and may perspire profusely.

Infrequently, these symptoms may be absent, and the occurrence of infarction can then be detected only by laboratory tests. Laboratory studies may show an elevation of the number of white blood cells in the blood or a rise in the enzyme content of the blood, indicating leakage from damaged heart muscle cells. The electrocardiogram (ECG) in most instances shows distinct and characteristic abnormalities at the onset, but the electrocardiographic abnormalities may be less characteristic or totally absent. The intensity of the symptoms depends on the size of the area of muscle affected by the heart attack.

In most persons who experience an acute myocardial infarction, the circulation remains adequate. Only by subtle evidence such as rales (abnormal respiratory sounds) in the lungs or a gallop rhythm of the heartbeat may the evidence of some minor degree of heart failure be detected. In a small percentage of cases, the state of shock occurs, with pallor, coolness of the hands and feet, low blood pressure, and rapid heart action. In these cases myocardial infarction is deadly, with low survival rates. Mortality is also related to age, for the process is more lethal in the elderly. In a small number of persons there may be thromboembolism (obstruction caused by a clot that has broken loose from its site of formation) into an artery elsewhere in the body.

In some individuals the damage caused by the infarction may interfere with the functioning of the mitral valve, the valve between the left upper and lower chambers, and result in a form of valvular heart disease. It may cause a rupture of the interventricular septum, the partition between the left and right ventricles, with the development of a ventricular septal defect, such as is seen in some forms of congenital heart disease. Rupture of the ventricle also may occur.

The focus of treatment is to limit the size of the area of tissue lost from lack of blood (infarct) and to prevent and treat complications, such as arrhythmia. Thus, the sooner the heart rate can be monitored by an ECG and the more promptly the arrhythmia is reversed by defibrillation with either antiarrhythmic drugs or electrical shock, the greater the chance of survival. Pain is treated with analgesics such as morphine, and rest and sedation are required. Other drugs that may be administered include beta-adrenergic-blocking drugs (beta-blockers) to relax the heart muscle, anticoagulants (e.g., heparin) to prevent clotting, fibrinolytic drugs to dissolve existing clots, and nitroglycerin to improve blood flow to the heart. Coronary thrombolysis therapy is widely used. It involves the administration of drugs such as streptokinase or tissue plasminogen activator (tPA) to prevent further blood clots from forming. Angioplasty or coronary artery bypass surgery are additional measures for patients requiring further treatment.

The prognosis for patients who survive a heart attack is generally favourable, depending on the degree of injury to the heart. Convalescence from an acute myocardial infarction may last several weeks, allowing time for scar tissue to form in the area of an infarction and for a gradual return to activity. Although some persons may have residual evidence of heart failure or other cardiac malfunction, most individuals may return to an active lifestyle after a period of weeks and are not in any way invalided by the process. These individuals do, however, have an increased potential for subsequent myocardial infarction.

Factors that contribute to the risk of heart attack include those that increase the risk of atherosclerosis, such as high blood pressure (hypertension), diabetes mellitus, increased blood levels of low-density lipoprotein (LDL) cholesterol, smoking, and a family history of the disease. Particularly vulnerable to atherosclerosis are middle-aged men and individuals with the hereditary disease hypercholesterolemia. Physicians often take all these measures into consideration when evaluating an individual's risk of heart disease and myocardial infarction.

Most heart attacks occur in the morning, a phenomenon that researchers have linked to circadian rhythm. In the morning hours, increasing circadian-driven secretion of certain hormones, particularly epinephrine, norepinephrine, and cortisol, triggers subsequent increases in oxygen demand and blood pressure. These factors in turn increase circulatory activity. In addition, the production of endothelial progenitor cells, which appear to play a crucial role in repairing the lining of blood vessels, also follows a circadian pattern, with fewer cells present in the circulation in the early morning. Decreased levels of these cells results in depressed endothelial maintenance, which scientists suspect may facilitate the onset of a heart attack upon waking.

SURVIVAL DURING AND AFTER A HEART ATTACK

The risk of death from an arrhythmia is greatest within the first few minutes of the onset of a blockage in a coronary artery or of acute ischemia (reduction of blood flow) occurring in the region of the heart muscle. Thus, of those likely to die during the first two weeks after a major heart attack, nearly half will die within one hour of the onset of symptoms.

During the first few hours most persons have some disturbances of rhythm and conduction. Ventricular fibrillation is particularly common in the first two hours, and its incidence decreases rapidly during the next 10 to 12 hours. If undetected, ventricular fibrillation is lethal. Once the patient has reached the hospital, fibrillation can be reversed in 80 to 90 percent of patients with the use of appropriate electronic devices for monitoring heart rhythm, for giving a direct-current shock to stop it, and for resuscitation. Given that the vast majority of heart attacks occur at home, treatment that allows for intervention in the first critical minutes holds the greatest hope of increasing survival rates. CPR training targeted to people that are most likely to witness a heart attack and the availability of automatic external defibrillators for use in a home setting by people with no medical training are common means of saving heart attack sufferers.

Both the immediate and the long-term outlook of persons after heart attack depends on the extent of myocardial damage and the influence of this damage on cardiac function. Efforts to limit or reduce the size of the infarct have been unsuccessful in improving the short- or long-term outlook. Procedures that cause thrombi (clots) to dissolve (thrombolysis), however, have led to the dramatic and immediate opening of apparently blocked coronary arteries. When such measures are implemented within four hours (and preferably within one hour) of the onset of a heart attack, the chances of survival are greater and the long-term prognosis is improved. Naturally occurring lytic enzymes (such as streptokinase) and genetically engineered products are used, as is aspirin.

SUDDEN DEATH

The term *sudden death* is used imprecisely and includes death that is almost instantaneous as well as death in which rapidly deteriorating disease processes may occupy as much as two or three days. In heart disease both may occur, but the term characteristically refers to instantaneous death, which is frequent in coronary heart disease. Sudden death from coronary heart disease occurs so frequently that less than half of the persons who die from heart attacks each year in the United States survive long enough to reach the hospital.

Instantaneous cardiac death is usually due to ventricular fibrillation (an uncontrolled and uncoordinated twitching of the ventricle muscle), with total mechanical inadequacy of the heart and erratic and ineffective electrical activity. Sudden death may occur without any previous manifestations of coronary heart disease. It may occur in the course of angina pectoris and causes about one-half of the deaths due to acute myocardial infarction in hospitalized patients, though this number is decreasing with the more widespread use of coronary care units. Although a reduced supply of blood to the heart undoubtedly is the precipitating factor, acute myocardial infarction does not always occur. In most persons who have died almost instantaneously, no infarction was present, but there was widespread coronary artery disease. In rare instances sudden death occurs without a major degree of coronary artery disease.

The use of cardiopulmonary resuscitation (CPR) coupled with electrical defibrillation (the use of electrical shocks), if applied within a few minutes of the sudden death episode, may successfully resuscitate the majority of patients. In coronary care units, where the facilities and trained personnel are immediately available, the percentage of successful resuscitations is high. In general hospitals where resuscitation teams have been established, the percentage is less satisfactory. Sudden death usually occurs outside the hospital, of course, and thus presents a more difficult problem. Mobile coronary care units responding as emergency ambulances improve a patient's chance of survival considerably, but effective resuscitation depends upon the prompt arrival of the unit. The use of drugs and other means to prevent the onset of sudden death has been relatively successful in the coronary care unit, except in situations in which the disease has been present for a long period of time.

PREVENTION OF CORONARY HEART DISEASE

To prevent heart disease, physicians recommend that patients quit smoking; eat a diet in which about 30 percent of the calories come from fat, choosing polyunsaturated fats and avoiding saturated fat and trans fat; reduce high blood pressure; increase physical activity; and maintain a weight within normal limits. Although the circumstantial evidence from many kinds of studies supporting these measures is impressive, not all these measures have been shown to be as effective as expected or predicted. Quitting smoking does lower the risk of cardiovascular disease. In fact, within a few years of quitting, patients show a risk factor for heart disease nearly equal to that of people who have never smoked. People with familial hypercholesterolemia (high cholesterol) benefit greatly from reduction of high levels of serum cholesterol. Rather surprisingly, studies suggest that even people who have borderline high cholesterol benefit from drugs that lower cholesterol. Results from studies in which participants modify their diet have had unexpected results, however, in that a low-fat diet does not seem to lead to reduced coronary risk. More studies on the effect of diet on heart disease are needed. And, although lowering blood cholesterol does have a great impact on heart disease, reducing high blood pressure has not been shown to lower coronary mortality as significantly.

DISEASES OF THE PULMONARY ARTERY AND AORTA

There exist several important acquired diseases of the pulmonary artery and aorta, including rheumatic heart disease, pulmonary heart disease (cor pulmonale), and aneurysm. These diseases are distinguished by their varied pathologies and causes. For example, rheumatic heart disease and syphilis of the heart are caused by infection with bacterial organisms, whereas cor pulmonale may arise from preexisting, chronic conditions, such as bronchitis or emphysema. In many instances, because of their distinct symptoms and causes, pulmonary artery and aortic diseases are readily diagnosed and treated.

RHEUMATIC HEART DISEASE

Rheumatic heart disease results from inflammation of the endocardium (heart lining), myocardium (heart muscle), and pericardium (the sac that surrounds the heart) that occurs during acute rheumatic fever, an infection with *Streptococcus pyogenes* organisms. The disease includes those later developments that persist after the acute process has subsided and that may result in damage to a valve, which may in turn lead to heart failure.

Rheumatic fever is poorly understood. The disease process occurs days or weeks following the initial streptococcal infection. Later infections may bring about recurrences of rheumatic fever that damage the heart. Immunologic processes (reactions to a foreign protein) are thought to be responsible for the response that damages the heart and particularly the heart valves. Rapid and effective treatment or prevention of streptococcal infections stops the acute process.

Many other factors of a geographic, economic, and climatic nature influence the incidence of rheumatic fever but are not the primary causes. Rheumatic fever became less common in the second half of the 20th century, and, with better control of streptococcal infections, there is an indication of a sharp decline in rheumatic heart disease.

It is thought that the basic pathologic lesion involves inflammatory changes in the collagen, the main supportive protein of the connective tissue. There is also inflammation of the endocardium and the pericardium. Only a relatively small percentage of deaths occur in the acute phase, with evidence of overwhelming inflammation associated with acute heart failure. There may be a disturbance of the conduction system of the heart and involvement of other tissues of the body, particularly the joints. About one-half of the persons found to have late rheumatic valvular disease give some indication that they have had acute rheumatic fever.

The major toll of rheumatic fever is in the deformity of the heart valves created by the initial attack or by

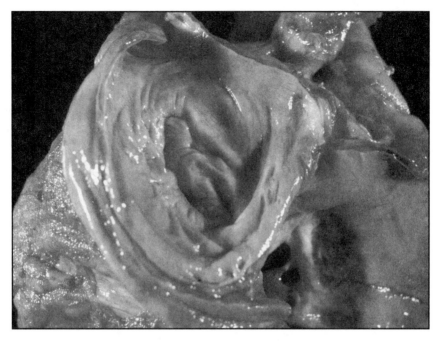

This section of a human heart shows stenosis of the mitral valve, which was caused by rheumatic fever. CNRI/Photo Researchers, Inc.

frequently repeated attacks of the acute illness. Although there may be valve involvement in the acute stages, it usually requires several years before valve defects become manifest as the cause of heart malfunction. The valve most frequently affected is the mitral valve, less commonly the aortic valve, and least common of all, the tricuspid valve. The lesion may cause either insufficiency of the valve, preventing it from operating in a normal fashion and leading to regurgitation, or stenosis (narrowing) of the valve, preventing a normal flow of blood and adding to the burden of the heart.

Mitral valve involvement is usually symptomless initially but may lead to left ventricular failure with shortness of breath. Heart murmurs are reasonably accurate signposts for specific valvular diagnoses. A murmur during the diastolic, or resting, phase of the heart, when blood normally flows through the mitral valve to fill the ventricle, generally indicates the presence of mitral stenosis. On the other hand, a murmur during systole, or contraction, of the left ventricle, indicates an abnormal flow of blood back through the mitral valve and into the left atrium (mitral regurgitation). When this latter condition is present, each beat of the heart must pump enough blood to supply the body as well as the wasted reflux into the pulmonary vascular system. This additional workload causes dilation and enlargement of the ventricle and leads to the development of congestive heart failure.

Involvement of the aortic valve is common, and again there may be evidence of stenosis or insufficiency. The presence of aortic stenosis may lead to a marked hypertrophy (enlargement) of the left ventricle of the heart. Involvement of either the tricuspid or pulmonic valve occurs in a similar fashion. In many persons with rheumatic valvular disease, more than one valve is involved. The specific type of valve involved influences the clinical picture of congestive failure.

Pulmonary Heart Disease (Cor Pulmonale)

In various lung diseases an obstruction to blood flow through the network of vessels in the lungs develops. This places a burden on the right side of the heart, which normally pumps against a low-pressure load with little resistance to blood flow. Pulmonary-artery pressures are normally low compared with those in the aorta.

Pulmonary heart disease may be divided into acute and chronic forms. The classic form of acute pulmonary heart disease (acute cor pulmonale) occurs when there is a sudden obstruction to the pulmonary blood-flow pattern, as occurs with a massive embolus—a blood clot that has broken loose from its point of formation. This impairs blood flow through the lungs, causes additional reflex changes that add to the heart's burden, and creates an acute form of high blood pressure in the pulmonary artery, with dilation and failure of the right ventricle. The right ventricle's pumping ability is acutely reduced, and, therefore, the amount of blood available for the left side of the heart is also restricted, so that systemic circulatory failure occurs. In acute cor pulmonale, the valve sounds from the pulmonic valve may be loud.

Chronic cor pulmonale, as distinguished from acute cor pulmonale, may be caused by a form of pulmonary disease—such as chronic bronchitis or emphysema—in which lung tissue is destroyed and replaced with air spaces, causing a loss of pulmonary blood vessels. Indeed, the most common cause of chronic cor pulmonale is often described as chronic obstructive pulmonary disease (COPD), a term used to refer to any condition in which the airflow is obstructed, as in chronic bronchitis and emphysema.

Chronic cor pulmonale also may be caused by multiple blood clots in the vessels of the lung or by a primary disorder of the pulmonary blood vessels. The result is a form of heart failure partly based on an obstruction to blood flow through the pulmonary vessels, producing high blood pressure in the pulmonary artery (pulmonary hypertension). Cyanosis may be evident, indicating that the arterial blood is not saturated with oxygen. In patients with chronic bronchitis and emphysema, the lack of oxygen contributes to pulmonary hypertension. The manifestations of heart failure are present—particularly where there is edema (the accumulation of fluid in tissues)—except that shortness of breath is often due to the underlying lung disease. The resultant back pressure on the right ventricle increases the work and the size of the chamber, leading to heart enlargement and eventually, if uncorrected, heart failure. In chronic cor pulmonale, there may be electro-cardiographic evidence of chronic strain on the right side of the heart.

A person with cor pulmonale has a chronic cough, experiences difficulty in breathing after exertion, wheezes, and is weak and easily fatigued. However, respiratory symptoms typically are not prominent, and the disorder in its early stages is not accompanied by edema in the lung. The clinical picture in the more severe form is one of shock, with cold, pale, and clammy skin, low arterial pressure, and a high pulse rate. Oxygen transfer in the lungs is severely impaired, and the heart may be acutely dilated.

Treatment of the acute form of the disease is often by removal of the pulmonary blockage, which often involves the administration of anticoagulant drugs (such as strep-tokinase) and oxygen, which relieve the hypoxia (low serum oxygen levels). In some instances, the obstruction may be removed surgically. Treatment of chronic cor pulmonale includes the use of antibiotics to combat respi-ratory infection, the restriction of sodium intake, and administration of diuretics and cardiovascular drugs such as digitalis or calcium channel blockers. In addition, drugs with anticoagulant effects can be useful in the treatment of chronic pulmonary heart disease. However, the course that affords the best chance of improvement in patients with cor pulmonale due to chronic bronchitis and emphy-sema includes prompt treatment of infection, termination of smoking, and correction of the lack of oxygen.

OTHER DISEASES OF THE PULMONARY ARTERY AND AORTA

Arteriosclerosis may involve the aorta and its major branches. Indeed, it seems to be an almost inevitable pro-cess with increasing age, but the rate of development and the extent of involvement vary greatly. The process may merely limit the elasticity of the aorta and allow for some dilation and increased complexity of the path of the blood flow as age advances. In more severe instances, there may be a major degree of dilation or localized formation of aneurysms (bulging of the vessel wall at a point of weakness), generally in the abdominal portion of the aorta. These aneurysms may result in pain and may occasionally rupture, causing sudden death. The arteriosclerotic process may impair the flow of blood to the tributaries of the aorta and lead to a variety of ischemic states—i.e., result in various types of damage that come from an insufficient supply of blood. This condition is particularly notable when the renal vessels are involved, creating a state of renal ischemia, occasionally creating hypertension, and possibly terminating in renal failure.

Medial necrosis is a lesion of the aorta in which the media (the middle coat of the artery) deteriorates, and, in association with arteriosclerosis and often hypertension, it may lead to a dissecting aneurysm. In a dissecting aneurysm a rupture in the intima, the innermost coat of the artery, permits blood to enter the wall of the aorta, causing separation of the layers of the wall. Obstruction to tributaries may occur, which is usually associated with severe chest pain. In many instances there is a secondary rupture of the exterior wall, which may lead to fatal internal bleeding. The aortic wall may become inflamed as an isolated process.

Calcium salts that deposit in the aorta wall may occur as a part of the arteriosclerotic process or of other disease involvement. In certain conditions, such as congenital heart disease, blood clots (thrombi) may form in the pulmonary artery, and these may break loose. Blood clots in the lungs (pulmonary emboli) may arise from this and other sources in the systemic venous circulation. These fragments of clot may be small, causing no detectable manifestations, or large, causing obstruction of either the total pulmonary arterial flow or of flow to an area of lung.

Aneurysm

As noted above, aneurysm is a widening of an artery that develops from a weakness or destruction of the medial layer of the blood vessel. Because of the constant pressure

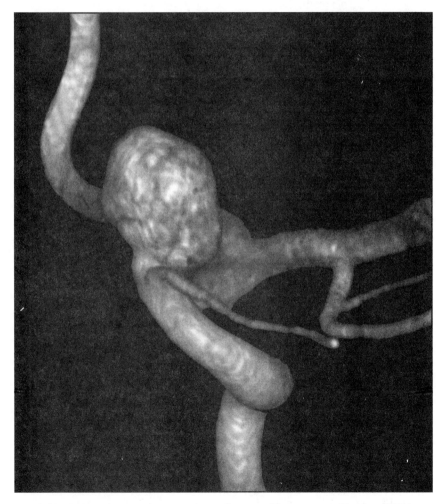

This image gives a close-up view of a carotid aneurysm. Zephyr/SPL/ Getty Images

of the circulating blood within the artery, the weakened part of the arterial wall becomes enlarged, leading ultimately to serious and even fatal complications from the compression of surrounding structures or from rupture and hemorrhage. Aneurysms may occur in any part of the aorta or major arteries. Usually caused by atherosclerosis (thickening of the arterial walls), aneurysms also may be the result of infection (such as syphilis), trauma, or congenital abnormalities.

The symptoms of an aneurysm vary with the extent of the defect and its location. A person with an aortic aneurysm may not have symptoms until the aneurysm enlarges beyond 5 or 6 cm (2 or 2.5 inches) in diameter. If an aneurysm in the chest presses against the windpipe and the bronchi, it can interfere with breathing and lead to coughing. Pain may occur in the back, front, or side and may radiate to the neck or shoulders. An abdominal aneurysm may cause pain in the abdomen or back that may radiate into the groin or upper thigh.

Diagnosis of an aneurysm is made by physical examination, X-ray, or imaging with ultrasound, computerized tomography (CT) scanning, magnetic resonance imaging (MRI), or aortography. The treatment of large aneurysms involves the surgical removal of the diseased segment and its replacement with an artificial artery made from a synthetic fibre such as Dacron™. Endovascular surgery is a less invasive procedure: a fine, meshlike tube (stent) covered with a graft of Dacron™ or some other plastic material is advanced to the site of the aneurysm in a catheter that has been inserted into a groin artery. Once in place, the stent is expanded by balloon dilation and the graft attached to the wall of the artery above and below the aneurysm, relieving the pressure on the weakened walls of the blood vessel.

Syphilis of the Heart and Aorta

Syphilis, a disease caused by infection with the micro-organism *Treponema pallidum*, is widespread in its early stages, affecting the entire body. During this initial phase there may be transient inflammation of the heart muscle, but usually with little or no impairment of the circulation. In the late stages of the disease, there may be syphilitic involvement of the heart, confined almost purely to the aorta and aortic valve. A particularly severe form of aortic insufficiency may develop, with subsequent dilation and enlargement of the heart and, eventually, heart failure. The disease process often involves the base of the aorta and the blood flow through the openings into the coronary vessels from the aorta, causing impairment of the coronary circulation, with resultant angina pectoris and, on rare occasions, myocardial infarction.

The syphilitic process may also involve the wall of the aorta. The result is the loss of the aorta's elastic properties, the dilation of the aorta, and, at times, the formation of aneurysms of the aorta. The aneurysms may become large and interfere with blood flow through the aortic tributaries in the involved area. They may be the source of pain and eventually may rupture, causing sudden death from loss of blood into the heart cavity. Syphilis of the aorta was common in the past, but, with the advent of more-modern control mechanisms, plus effective early treatment with the use of penicillin, the disorder has become much less common. Late complications can be effectively avoided with early antisyphilitic treatment.

CHAPTER 5

DISEASES OF HEART TISSUES, DISTURBANCES IN CARDIAC RHYTHM, AND HEART FAILURE

D iseases of the endocardium and valve tissues of the heart can result in acute and severe cardiovascular dysfunction. Likewise, abnormalities of the heart's natural pacemaker or of the nerves that conduct its impulses can give rise to disordered cardiac rhythm, or arrhythmia. Heart failure may result from a number of the aforementioned disorders, as well as from a host of other conditions that cause the heart muscle to fail to contract and relax properly. Heart failure may affect the left or the right side of the heart, and in an individual affected by failure of both ventricles, the resultant enlarged heart produces a distinct three-beat heartbeat.

Diseases of the heart tissues involving infectious organisms require rapid diagnosis and treatment in order to prevent long-term damage to heart function. Similarly, the prompt diagnosis of disturbances in cardiac rhythm, as well as early detection of disorders underlying heart failure is central to the effective treatment of these conditions.

DISEASES OF HEART TISSUES

Diseases of heart tissues may involve inflammation of the endocardium (the tissue lining the inner surface of the heart), the myocardium (the muscular tissue of the heart), or the pericardium (the tissue layer covering the heart). The heart also may be affected by any of a considerable number of collagen diseases. Collagen is the principal connective-tissue protein, and thus diseases of collagen are generally referred to as diseases of the connective tissues.

Diseases of heart tissues arise from diverse causes. For example, whereas some diseases of heart tissue are due to the presence of an infectious organism, others may be caused by abnormalities in structures such as the valves that control the flow of blood through the heart chambers. Thus, while some of these conditions are easily treated through the administration of antibiotic agents, others may require surgical correction.

DISEASES OF THE ENDOCARDIUM AND VALVES

Bacterial endocarditis—a disease in which bacterial or fungal infection becomes established on the surface of a heart valve or, less commonly, in a blood vessel wall or in the endocardium (inner lining) of the heart—usually occurs where there has been some previous lesion, either congenital or acquired. Most frequently the location is at the line of closure of the valve.

The disease may be acute and severe, or it may be chronic, often referred to as subacute bacterial endocarditis. It may erode the valve structure, or it may be of an inflammatory nature, producing nodules with the ulcerative surface of active infection. Because the bacteria are embedded in the lesion, the blood's normal immune defenses have difficulty entering into play. For this reason, certain types of bacterial endocarditis become more chronic and more slowly progressive.

The effects of the lesion are complex, being related to the presence of a bacterial infection in the body, local damage to the valve, and systemic damage caused by fragments of a blood clot that breaks off and travels through the bloodstream to distant organs. These clots cause infarctions or abscesses, a type of kidney disease, and other small areas of bleeding and necrosis in the skin, eyes, and other parts of the body.

Before the advent of antibiotic therapy, bacterial endocarditis was almost always a fatal disease. Many affected persons can now be successfully treated, given the best conditions, though the mortality rate still remains relatively high. Inflammation of the heart lining, such as endocarditis that is not caused by infection, may occur in some illnesses, but it does not result in the formation and breaking loose of blood clots.

In the course of rheumatoid arthritis, a chronic inflammation of the joints of unknown cause, a type of valvular damage has been recognized. It is different from that caused by rheumatic fever but leads to valvular insufficiency and stenosis (narrowing) in much the same fashion and is particularly likely to attack the aortic valve. The tendencies toward heart failure and toward impairment of heart function are the same as in rheumatic valvular disease.

Aortic Insufficiency

Aortic insufficiency is a failure of the valve at the mouth of the aorta to prevent backflow of blood from the aorta into the left ventricle of the heart, from which it has been pumped. The defect causes characteristic heart sounds, audible through a stethoscope. Affected persons may experience difficulty in breathing after mild physical exertion and may suffer spasms of difficult breathing while resting in bed. Congestive heart failure—the effects of the heart's inability to function adequately as a pump—may develop.

Aortic insufficiency may result from a congenitally defective valve, from rheumatic heart disease, or from syphilis. Medical treatment is directed toward management of the congestive heart failure; prevention of the recurrence of rheumatic heart disease; and prevention of bacterial endocarditis, bacterial invasion of the heart lining. Surgical treatment consists in replacing the diseased valve with a synthetic substitute or a transplant.

Aortic Stenosis

Aortic stenosis is a narrowing of the passage between the left ventricle of the heart and the aorta. The defect is most often in the valve at the mouth of the aorta but may be just above or below the valve (supravalvular and subvalvular aortic stenosis, respectively). Aortic stenosis in a person younger than 20 years of age is usually congenital in origin. If it appears during middle age, it is most often the result of rheumatic heart disease. Aortic stenosis in elderly persons may be the result of degeneration of the valve with age. Most patients are male.

Aortic stenosis causes characteristic heart sounds, audible through a stethoscope. Affected persons may faint after exertion or may experience the chest pain known as angina pectoris. The stenosis may bring about congestive heart failure—the effects of the heart's inability to function adequately as a pump. Medical treatment is directed toward the angina pectoris and heart failure and toward prevention of bacterial invasion of the heart lining (endocarditis). Surgical treatment consists in repairing the aortic valve or replacing it with a synthetic substitute or a transplant.

Mitral Insufficiency

Mitral insufficiency, also called mitral regurgitation, is an inability of the mitral valve to prevent the flow of blood back from the left ventricle into the left atrium. Normally, the valve permits blood to flow from the atrium to the ventricle but prevents its return. Most often, the inability of the mitral valve to close adequately is caused by scarring from rheumatic heart disease. It may also be due to a congenital defect of the valve or may arise from defects in the muscles and tendons (the papillary muscles and chordae tendineae) that operate the valve. Less frequently it may be due to endocarditis or cardiac tumour. The condition is recognized from characteristic heart sounds and from patterns that show up in echocardiography or electrocardiography.

Persons with mitral insufficiency may not be conscious of any effect of the condition or may be easily fatigued and may experience difficulty in breathing after exertion or while lying down. The left atrium may become greatly enlarged, and left ventricular failure eventually develops.

Medical treatment is restriction of vigorous exercise, reduction of sodium intake and increase in sodium excretion, and administration of anticoagulants to avoid the formation of blood clots in the veins. Some persons with severe defects are treated surgically by replacement of the valve.

Mitral Stenosis

Mitral stenosis is a narrowing of the mitral valve that is usually a result of rheumatic fever, though, rarely, the narrowed valve is a congenital defect. The condition, most common in women under 45, is diagnosed by recognition of typical heart sounds and confirmed by certain patterns that appear in echocardiography or electrocardiography.

Narrowing of the valve increases pressure in the left atrium and in the pulmonary veins and capillaries (oxygenated blood from the lungs enters the left atrium by way of the pulmonary veins). The increased pressure in the pulmonary vessels may lead to congestion of the lungs and the collection of fluid in the pulmonary tissues. Difficulty in breathing, particularly after exercise, is one consequence. If the small vessels of the lungs develop resistance, possibly by the thickening of their walls, accumulation of fluid in the lungs decreases, but increased back pressure in the right ventricle of the heart (from which blood is pumped to the lungs) may lead to early failure of the right side of the heart.

Atrial fibrillation, or uncontrolled and irregular twitching of the upper chambers of the heart, occurs in most persons who have mitral stenosis. Another possible complication is the development of blood clots in the left atrium; these may break loose and travel through the arteries to the kidneys, the spleen, the legs, or the brain, obstructing blood flow at those points with consequent death of tissue.

Medical treatment includes the regulation of exercise so as to avoid fatigue and to minimize difficulty in breathing; reduction of sodium intake and increase in sodium excretion to reduce accumulation of fluids in the tissues;

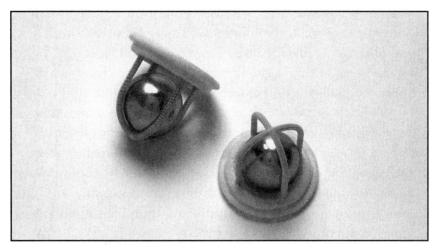

Heart valves made of metal and plastic can be implanted into patients with diseased valves. This ball and cage design was the first effective artificial valve to be successfully implanted in humans. SSPL via Getty Images

and administration of anticoagulants to reduce the possibility of clot formation. Surgical treatment is replacement of the valve with one of Dacron ™, stainless steel, or some other special material, or with a transplant of a valve from a pig heart.

Diseases of the Myocardium

There has been increasing recognition of a type of heart disease characterized as primary myocardial disease. The cardiomyopathies are diseases involving the myocardium itself. They include any cardiac disease process that results in heart failure due to a decrease in the pumping power of the heart or due to an impairment in the filling of the cardiac chambers. Cardiomyopathies are unique in that they are not the result of hypertensive, congenital, valvular, or pericardial diseases and are rarely the result of ischemic heart disease. This form of heart disease is often sufficiently distinctive, both in general symptoms and in patterns of blood flow, to allow a diagnosis to be made. Increasing awareness of the condition, along with improved diagnostic techniques, has shown that cardiomyopathy is a major cause of morbidity and mortality. In some areas of the world, it may account for as many as 30 percent of all deaths due to heart disease.

A large number of cardiomyopathies are apparently not related to an infectious process but are not well understood. A number of these are congenital and many cause enlargement of the heart. About one-third of these diseases are familial, and some of these are transmitted as a non-sex-linked autosomal dominant trait (i.e., a person may be affected if he inherits the tendency from one parent). They are particularly common among African Americans.

A number of metabolic diseases associated with endocrine disorders may cause cardiomyopathies. Other metabolic disorders that may contribute to cardiomyopathy include beriberi, caused by a nutritional deficiency, and a form of cardiomyopathy seen in chronic alcoholics. Cardiomyopathies can also be caused by cobalt poisoning, which is sometimes seen in workers exposed to pigments. There are also rare cardiomyopathies caused by drugs. Infections, such as acute rheumatic fever and several viral infections, may cause any of a number of types of myocarditis. Myocarditis may also occur as a manifestation of a generalized hypersensitivity (allergic or immunologic) reaction throughout the body. However, despite knowledge about these causes, the instances in which the underlying cause of cardiomyopathy is actually identified are few. In fact, the majority of cardiomyopathies are idiopathic, or of unknown cause.

Cardiomyopathies are referred to as being either primary or secondary in nature, based on whether or not a cause is identified. Primary cardiomyopathies are those in which the basic disease involves the myocardium rather than other heart structures, and the cause of the disease is not known and not part of a disorder of other organs. In secondary cardiomyopathies, the cause of the myocardial abnormality is known, and the cardiomyopathy is a manifestation of a systemic disease process. Clinically, the cardiomyopathies fall into three categories: dilated cardiomyopathy; hypertrophic cardiomyopathy; and restrictive cardiomyopathy.

Dilated cardiomyopathy, the most common type of the disease, is characterized by an enlarged heart with stretching of the ventricle (lower chamber) and atrium (upper chamber). The left ventricle, which pumps oxygenated blood to the body tissues, shows weakness in contraction (systolic dysfunction) and stiffness in expansion and filling (diastolic dysfunction). These dysfunctions lead to fluid retention and eventually heart failure. Preceding heart attack is known to cause the condition, as is exposure to toxic substances such as alcohol, cobalt, and some anticancer drugs.

In hypertrophic cardiomyopathy, the ventricles are quite small owing to abnormal growth and arrangement of the cardiac muscle fibres. This form of the disease is often hereditary and has been associated with mutations in several different genes, each of which encodes a protein necessary for the formation of sarcomeres, the contractile units of muscle. However, mutations in two genes, *MYBPC3* (myosin-binding protein C, cardiac) and

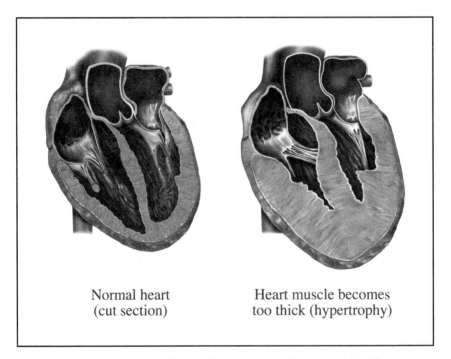

Normal heart
(cut section)

Heart muscle becomes
too thick (hypertrophy)

This diagram compares a healthy heart to one with hypertrophy. Nucleus Medical Art, Inc./Getty Images

MYH7 (myosin, heavy chain 7, cardiac muscle, beta), are responsible for roughly 80 percent of familial hypertrophic cardiomyopathy cases. The onset of symptoms in people affected by this form of the disease varies, ranging from infancy to late adulthood. Thickening, or hypertrophy, of the ventricular walls results in an extremely stiff heart, and subsequent impairment of the filling of the ventricles causes pressure to rise in the heart and lungs. The increased pressure in turn leads to shortness of breath and fluid retention. Hypertrophic cardiomyopathies are commonly associated with serious arrhythmias and sudden cardiac death.

Restrictive cardiomyopathy also is characterized by a stiff heart and impaired ventricular filling. In this case the abnormality is caused by the presence of fibrous (scar) tissue introduced by a disease such as amyloidosis. Patients display many of the symptoms of hypertrophic cardiomyopathy.

Some cardiomyopathies are associated with few symptoms and may be diagnosed only by electrocardiography, which can detect evidence of an enlarged heart and disturbances in cardiac conduction mechanisms. In other instances, extensive involvement may lead to heart failure. Many cardiomyopathies cause excess fluid retention, resulting in congestion of the lungs, and symptoms of weakness, fatigue, and shortness of breath. Sometimes affected persons develop a potentially fatal arrhythmia, or abnormal heart rhythm. Some cases may be chronic, with exacerbations and remissions over a period of years.

Treatment of cardiomyopathy is directed first toward identifying the underlying disease (e.g., hypothyroidism or hypertension). Patients are treated as any patient with heart failure. Indeed, all patients with heart failure have some sort of cardiomyopathy. If general treatment

measures fail, patients with cardiomyopathy can sometimes be helped with heart transplantation. Because some
forms of cardiomyopathy are inherited, individuals from
families with a history of the disease are encouraged to
have physical examinations, electrocardiograms, and
echocardiograms done periodically. In the future, genetic
screening may make it possible to detect persons at risk
for developing familial forms of cardiomyopathy.

DISEASES OF THE PERICARDIUM

Pericardial disease may occur as an isolated process or as a
subordinate and unsuspected manifestation of a disease
elsewhere in the body. Acute pericarditis—inflammation
of the pericardium—may result from invasion of the pericardium by one of a number of agents (viral, fungal,
protozoal), as a manifestation of certain connective-tissue
and allergic diseases, or as a result of chemical or metabolic
disturbances. Cancer and specific injury to the pericardium are also potential causes of pericardial disease.

Pain is the most common symptom in acute pericarditis,
though pericarditis may occur without pain. A characteristic sound, called friction rub, and characteristic
electrocardiographic findings are factors in diagnosis.
Acute pericarditis may be accompanied by an outpouring
of fluid into the pericardial sac. The presence of pericardial fluid in excessive amounts may enlarge the silhouette
of the heart in X-rays but not impair its function. If the
pericardial fluid accumulates rapidly or in great amounts,
if there is a hemorrhage into the sac, or if the pericardium
is diseased so that it does not expand, the heart is compressed, a state called cardiac tamponade. There is
interference with the heart's ability to fill with blood and
reduction of cardiac output. In its more severe form,

cardiac tamponade causes a shocklike state that may be lethal. Removal of the fluid is lifesaving in an emergency and aids in the identification of the cause.

Chronic constrictive pericarditis, caused by scar tissue in the pericardium, restricts the activity of the ventricles. In many instances the cause is not known, but in some it is the result of tuberculosis or other specific infections. It is treated most effectively by surgery. Tumours that either arise directly from the pericardium or are secondary growths from other sources may impair cardiac function and cause pericardial effusion (escape of fluid into the pericardium).

DISTURBANCES IN CARDIAC RHYTHM AND CONDUCTION

Disturbances in cardiac rhythm arise from conditions that affect the transmission of electrical impulses controlling heart rate and strength of contraction of the heart muscle. Many of these conditions alter the function of the "excitable," or conducting, cells of the heart muscle. This ultimately gives rise to arrhythmias, or abnormalities, in cardiac rhythm. In many instances, arrhythmias have few long-term effects on the health of the heart. However, in combination with other cardiovascular conditions, arrhythmias may seriously threaten heart function.

There are several different types of arrhythmias, and these are characterized generally by a fast heart rate (tachycardia) or by a slow heart rate (bradycardia). In some instances tachycardia and bradycardia may be normal, resulting from exercise or following a period of rest, respectively. However, there exist several disturbances in cardiac rhythm that may arise from sporadic or chronic dysfunction of the conducting cells controlling

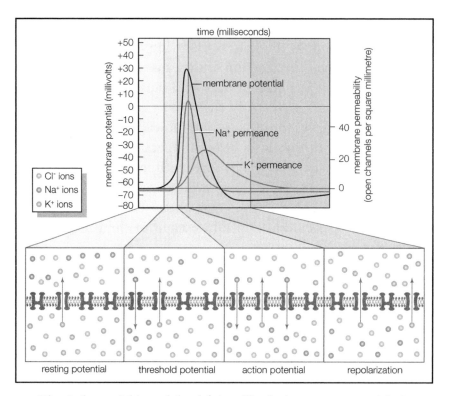

Electrical potential is graded at left in millivolts, ion permeance at right in open channels per square millimetre. At the resting potential, the membrane potential is close to EK, the equilibrium potential of K+. When sodium channels open, the membrane depolarizes. When depolarization reaches the threshold potential, it triggers an action potential. Generation of the action potential brings the membrane potential close to ENa, the equilibrium potential of Na+. When sodium channels close (lowering Na+ permeance) and potassium channels open (raising K+ permeance), the membrane repolarizes. Encyclopædia Britannica, Inc.

the rate of atrial contraction or the rate of ventricular contraction.

Severe rhythm disturbances include atrial fibrillation or ventricular fibrillation, conditions characterized by the arrival of chaotic electrical impulses that cause the heart to beat ineffectively at a very high rate. In many cases, abnormalities in cardiac rhythm and conduction can be corrected by drugs or by devices such as pacemakers that function to regulate the transmission of electrical impulses in the heart.

DETERMINANTS OF CARDIAC RHYTHM

The cardiac muscle cell is a type of "excitable" cell, meaning that it is capable of conducting electrical impulses that stimulate the heart muscle to contract. Excitable cells, which also include neurons and muscle cells, possess a unique ability to sense differences in voltage across their cell membrane. This transmembrane voltage gradient arises from the presence of ion-specific voltage-sensitive channels that are made up of proteins and are embedded in the lipid layers of the cell membrane. As their name implies, voltage-sensitive channels respond to changes in voltage (excitation) that lead to depolarization of the cell. When a cell is excited, each channel opens and transports specific ions (i.e., potassium [K], sodium [Na], calcium [Ca], and chloride [Cl]) from one side of the membrane to the other, often exchanging one ion species for a different ion species (i.e., the Na^+/K^+ ATPase channel transports three sodium ions out in exchange for two potassium ions pumped into the cell). Ion exchange is required for depolarization, reestablishing intracellular homeostasis, and cell repolarization.

Once the cell returns to its resting state (periods of time between electrical impulses when the cell is repolarized), voltage-sensitive channels close, and the cell is ready to receive another impulse. Cardiac cells at rest are fully repolarized when the intracellular environment reaches a specific negative charge (approximately −90 millivolts) relative to the extracellular environment (approximately 0 millivolt). The cycle of depolarization and repolarization in the heart is known as the cardiac action potential and occurs approximately 60 times every minute. In addition,

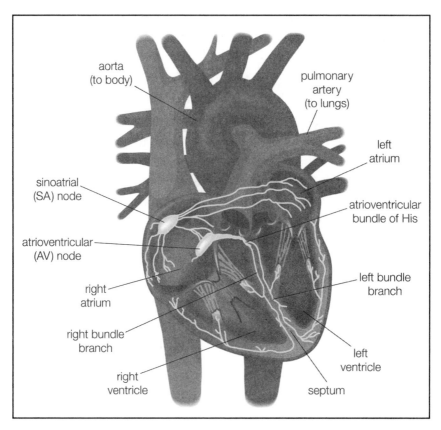

Electrical conduction in the heart in healthy individuals is controlled by pacemaker cells in the sinoatrial node. Electrical impulses are conducted from the sinoatrial node to the atrioventricular node and bundle of His, through the bundle branches, and into the ventricles. Encyclopædia Britannica, Inc.

cardiac muscle cells are unique from other types of excitable cells in that they remain permeable to potassium in the resting state. This facilitates the intracellular response to depolarization and, in combination with other potassium channels, ensures proper duration between and during action potentials.

Normal cardiac muscle cells do not spontaneously depolarize. For this reason, cardiac rhythm is dependent upon specialized conduction cells, called pacemaker cells, to generate the initiating impulse for depolarization.

These cells contain a complement of channels that aid in the generation of a rhythmic, spontaneous depolarization that initiates excitation. In healthy individuals, heart rate (impulse generation) is controlled by the pacemaker cells of the sinoatrial node. Under pathological conditions, and with some pharmacological interventions, other pacemakers elsewhere in the heart may become dominant. The rate at which the sinoatrial node produces electrical impulses is determined by the autonomic nervous system. As a result, heart rate increases in response to increased sympathetic nervous system activity, which is also associated with conditions that require increased cardiac output (i.e., exercise or fear). In contrast, the parasympathetic nervous system slows heart rate.

Once the electrical impulse is generated in the sinoatrial node, it is propagated rapidly throughout the heart. Specialized connections between conduction cells in the heart allow the electrical impulse to travel rapidly from the atria to the atrioventricular node and bundle of His (known as the atrioventricular junctional tissue), through the bundle branches and Purkinje fibres (known as the ventricular conduction system), and into the ventricular muscle cells that ultimately generate cardiac output. The conduction system in the atria is poorly defined but clearly designed to initiate atrial depolarization, as well as to propagate the impulse toward the ventricle. The atrioventricular node and bundle of His represent important supraventricular control points in the heart that distribute impulses to the ventricles via the right and left bundle branches. The impulse proceeds through the ventricular conduction system and into specialized conduction tissue in the subendocardial (innermost) layer of the ventricle. This tissue propagates impulses that travel from the inner wall to the outer wall of the heart. The atrioventricular node is also under autonomic control, through which sympathetic stimulation facilitates conduction and parasympathetic stimulation slows conduction. Abnormalities in this conduction system often create cardiac rhythm disturbances.

PREMATURE CONTRACTIONS

While vulnerable to pathological, physiological, and pharmacological stressors, cardiac rhythm control is remarkably constant and robust. Many people develop abnormalities in this system that have little pathological consequence. While the sinoatrial node pacemaker is dominant, occasional spontaneous premature beats may arise anywhere in the conduction system. Depending on their origin, they are described as premature atrial contractions, premature nodal contractions, or premature ventricular contractions. They typically do not interfere with normal cardiovascular function and are seen more frequently under circumstances of increased excitability and impulse generation, such as that occurring with physiological stress, stimulants (e.g., caffeine), and certain drugs. While they may be benign and of no physiological consequence, they may also be harbingers of more-serious cardiac abnormalities.

ARRHYTHMIA

Any variation from the normal rate or regularity of the heartbeat, usually resulting from irregularities within the conduction system of the heart, is known as an arrhythmia. Arrhythmias occur in both normal and diseased hearts and have no medical significance in and of themselves, although they may endanger heart function when coupled with other cardiac abnormalities.

Types of arrhythmias include tachycardia, which is a regular acceleration of the heart rate; bradycardia, a regular slowing of the heart rate; and premature atrial or ventricular beats, which are extra contractions within otherwise normal heart rhythm. While occasional irregularities are normal, prolonged or chronic arrhythmias associated with some forms of heart disease may reduce cardiac output, lowering blood pressure and affecting the perfusion of vital organs with blood, and can precipitate heart failure. Severe arrhythmias can trigger atrial fibrillation or ventricular fibrillation, in which the heart beats ineffectively at many times its normal rate.

Arrhythmias reflect the failure of the sinoatrial node, the normal cardiac pacemaker, to maintain a regular heartbeat, usually because of defects in the various pathways by which electrical impulses are carried to different areas of the heart. Anatomical defects or disease can slow down or speed up the propagation of electrical impulses, causing them to arrive out of the normal rhythm, or can turn the impulses back on their path, short-circuiting the pacemaker. Many arrhythmias can be corrected through physical methods, such as artificial pacemakers, defibrillators, and radiofrequency ablation (the application of radiofrequency energy to the area of the heart that is causing the arrhythmia), or by drugs such as beta-blockers (beta-adrenergic blocking agents, which are drugs that diminish excitatory response) and calcium channel blockers.

Tachycardia

Tachycardia is characterized as a heart rate of more than 100 beats per minute. It occurs normally during and after exercise or during emotional stress and represents no danger to healthy individuals. In some cases, however, tachycardia occurs without apparent cause or as a complication of a heart attack or heart disease and is an arrhythmia—i.e., a pathological deviation from the normal heartbeat rhythm. Most arrhythmias are caused by irregularities in the electrical stimuli that cause the heart to beat. Normally these pacemaking stimuli originate in the sinoatrial node. The chief symptoms of tachycardia are fatigue, faintness, dizziness, shortness of breath, and a sensation of thumping or palpitation in the chest.

Tachycardia can be terminated by administering an electrical shock to the heart to restore regular heart rhythm or by the administration of such antiarrhythmic drugs as lidocaine, procainamide, or quinidine.

Supraventricular Arrhythmia

Rhythm disturbances in the atrium can occur as a result of increased or decreased conduction rate, both of which may potentially compromise cardiac function. The electro-physiologic mechanisms for these changes are important with respect to prognosis and treatment.

Supraventricular tachycardia is initiated in the atria and arises from a number of conditions, including an increase in sinoatrial node impulse rate that normally occurs during conditions of high excitation, such as hyperthyroidism or exercise. Referred to as physiologically appropriate sinus tachycardia, this response stems from a demand for increased cardiac output. In contrast, pathological tachycardia is defined by its presence under circumstances where it is physiologically inappropriate. In some cases, symptoms may go unnoticed or cause slight increases in heart rate, such as in paroxysmal (sudden) supraventricular tachycardia, which occurs in many people as a relatively benign increase in heart rate, ranging anywhere from 160 to 240 beats per minute. This condition is easily controlled by a variety of physical or pharmacological approaches and can be prevented or reduced with beta blockers or calcium channel blocking agents. Some conditions, however, require more aggressive pharmaco-logical intervention or pacemaker implantation.

Atrial flutter (rapid atrial beat) may occur suddenly and unpredictably or may be a chronic sustained arrhythmia. The heart rate in atrial flutter approximates 300 beats per minute and is difficult to treat pharmacologically. In general, only a fraction of the atrial beats (one-third to one-fourth) are transmitted to the ventricle, which is done in a systematic manner so that the ventricular rate appears constant. Atrial flutter can also occur as a variant of paroxysmal supraventric-ular tachycardia in overdose of digitalis, which causes the atria to beat faster than the ventricles because atrial trans-mission to the ventricles is blocked. Patients with atrial flutter are susceptible to marked increases in heart rate with relatively little stimulation unless treated pharmacologically with beta-adrenergic blocking agents, digitalis, or calcium channel blocking agents. The sustained condition of atrial flutter is treated with electric countershock followed by anti-arrhythmic therapy to maintain normal rhythm. In many patients with chronic atrial flutter, the rhythm ultimately changes to atrial fibrillation, a chaotic disorganization of the atrial muscle in which multiple and organized electrical impulses arise.

Tachycardias that are sometimes resistant to treat-ment may arise from a series of abnormalities called Wolff-Parkinson-White syndrome. This syndrome is characterized by the presence of an alternative conduc-tion source from atrium to ventricle that bypasses the atrioventricular node, causing impulses to reach the ven-tricle too soon. A variety of tachycardias can occur under these circumstances that may be very rapid and life-threatening. Catheter ablation, in which the electrical conduction pathway is destroyed in the problematic cells, has been used to treat severe cases of this syndrome.

Atrial Fibrillation

Atrial fibrillation is an irregular rhythm of contraction of the muscles of the atrium. In some cases the fibrillations are not noticed by the patient, but frequently the chaotic, rapid, and shallow beats are felt as significant palpitations of the heart, often accompanied by shortness of breath, dizziness, and fatigue. Atrial fibrillation is the most common type of cardiac arrhythmia. It is not necessarily a serious condition in itself and need not result in significant restriction of activity. Nevertheless, its presence may create problems for other cardiac functions, particularly in the ventricles, since a small fraction of impulses are transmitted to the ventricles in an unpredictable manner In this case, the heart rate is described as irregularly irregular.

Atrial fibrillation arises when muscle cells in the wall of the atrium go through changes that interfere with the proper propagation of electrical nerve impulses. It is known to occur more frequently as the amount of fibrous tissue increases in the aging heart. There is also a significant familial propensity to the condition. Atrial fibrillation can also be brought on by other cardiac conditions that increase the load on the atrium, such as mitral valve disease and chronic congestive heart failure. Finally, atrial fibrillation may occur transiently as a result of overstimulation (as in hyperthyroidism) or irritation (as in pericarditis).

Atrial fibrillation interrupts the normal functioning of the sinoatrial node, which as mentioned is a mass of specialized muscle tissue in the right atrium that is the primary source of the impulses which serve as the natural pacemaker of the heart. Thus, not only is atrial rhythm disturbed but also the impulses activating the ventricles, which pump blood to the lungs and body. The ventricles are protected by the atrioventricular node from the extraordinary bombardment of impulses originating in the fibrillating atrium. However, people with atrial fibrillation, upon exercise or stress, frequently experience excessive increases in heart rate that must be treated with beta-blockers, calcium channel blockers, or digitalis.

In addition, atrial fibrillation can worsen the condition of cardiac patients whose ventricular functions are already impaired by heart failure or thickening of the ventricular walls (ventricular hypertrophy) by eliminating the secondary ventricular filling energy provided by a normally contracting left atrium. The most prevalent complication of atrial fibrillation results from the formation of blood clots in the wall of the fibrillating left atrium. These clots frequently break off into the circulation, where they may form emboli that can block arterial beds, thus causing substantial tissue damage. It is estimated that 25 percent of people with chronic atrial fibrillation ultimately will suffer a major embolism and stroke if they are not treated with anticoagulants such as warfarin (Coumadin).

Atrial fibrillation may have severe consequences that require various approaches to treatment. The primary strategy for treating atrial fibrillation is to address the underlying abnormality. Fibrillations can be interrupted by administering electric shocks to the ventricles, though in most cases this treatment must be followed by drug therapy to maintain a normal rhythm. Recent progress in clinical electrophysiology has offered the promise of a technique in which aberrant pacemakers can be ablated by ultrasound delivered through a catheter in order to provide stable defibrillation in some patients. However, in many cases, atrial fibrillation persists or recurs, and patients with chronic atrial fibrillation require treatment with the anticoagulant and antiarrhythmic drugs mentioned above.

Bradycardia

Bradycardia is characterized by slowing of the heart rate to 60 beats per minute or less. A slow heart rate in itself may have little medical significance; bradycardia is frequent among young adults, especially in highly trained athletes or during sleep. However, bradycardia may indicate significant heart disease if accompanied by other symptoms.

Bradycardia can arise from two general mechanisms. The sinoatrial node may not function properly either as a result of slow generation of impulses or of blocking of the propagation of impulses. As a result, other pacemakers in the heart become responsible for impulse generation, and these have intrinsically slower rates. The condition, while not harmful in and of itself, is usually an indication of problems with the atrial conduction system and frequently results in the development of atrial fibrillation. This form of bradycardia often produces weakness, confusion, and palpitations. In some circumstances, paroxysmal supraventricular tachycardia will abruptly terminate, and the sinoatrial node will not take up normal sinus rhythm. This is known as tachycardia-bradycardia syndrome. This syndrome belongs to a group of conditions described as sick sinus syndrome, in which slowing alternates with rapid acceleration of the heart rate. Sick sinus syndrome can result in a profound bradycardia that may cause fainting (syncope).

Another common cause of bradycardia, the blockage of electrical conduction through the atrioventricular node (heart block), is similar in its symptoms to sinus bradycardia. Bradycardia can also be produced by drugs such as digitalis or morphine and is a common abnormality in heart attack victims, for whom it often indicates a favourable prognosis. When bradycardia is accompanied by congestive heart failure or other serious complications, an artificial pacemaker may be necessary to regulate the heart rate.

Heart Block

Another mechanism for slow ventricular rates is heart block. Heart block arises from a lack of synchronization in the contractions of the atria and the ventricles. The lack of synchronization may range from a slight delay in the ventricular contractions to total heart block, a complete lack of synchronization between the atria and the ventricles. A characteristic of heart block is that the ventricles contract more slowly than the atria. Under these circumstances the sinoatrial node generates an appropriate impulse rate, but the impulses are not transmitted properly through the atrioventricular node and the His bundle.

Heart block is classified as first-degree (normal heart rate but delayed transmission of atrial impulse to ventricle), second-degree (only some atrial beats are transmitted to the ventricle), or third-degree (no transmission from the atrium to the ventricle occurs). In some cases, first-degree heart block may be a side effect of medication (i.e., digitalis). Treatment is not required for first-degree heart block, as it is a benign condition with a generally good prognosis. If heart block progresses into severe second-degree or third-degree stages, a pacemaker is implanted for proper function.

Heart block is caused by disease of some portion of the pathway over which the contractive impulse travels through the heart. This may occur as a result of severe injury, such as heart attack, in which an emergency pacemaker may be implanted. However, it frequently occurs as a function of normal aging because of fibrosis of the His bundle. Third-degree heart block initiated in the His bundle results in a very slow heart rate and almost always requires a pacemaker, which regulates heart action by means of minute electric shocks. Third-degree heart block can also occur from blocks of the atrioventricular node in patients with congenital heart block. These patients are generally asymptomatic and capable of maintaining cardiac output under most circumstances. This is because the presence of other, more rapid, pacemaker cells below the level of the block is sensitive to metabolic demand, allowing some increase in heart rate. The use of pacemakers in patients with congenital heart block is not usually required. In addition, the rate of impulses that regulate ventricular contractions can be increased by the administration of certain drugs for some patients with heart block.

Ventricular Arrhythmia

Ventricular arrhythmias represent the major mechanism of cardiac sudden death, which is a leading cause of death in the United States, where each year more than 325,000 people die suddenly. Almost all of these deaths are related to ventricular fibrillation. While this rhythm disturbance may be associated with heart attack, evidence suggests that more than half are not related to heart attack.

The mechanism by which ventricular arrhythmias occur is not completely understood. One basic mechanism appears to result from spontaneous generation of cardiac impulses within the ventricle. It is not clear whether this condition results from pathologically altered ventricular cells or from cells in the specialized conduction system.

A second mechanism of ventricular arrhythmia is associated with reentry of an impulse. In this situation, slowed impulse conduction in the ventricle leads to the generation of ectopic impulses (electrical impulses derived from an area of the heart other than the sinus node) that are primarily the result of temporal dispersion of the impulse between adjacent areas of the ventricle. This sets up an electrical impulse circuit within the ventricle that may progress into an arrhythmia.

Reentry mechanisms are important components of ventricular arrhythmias and may be as simple as a premature ventricular beat coupled to a normal beat or as serious as a dangerous ventricular tachycardia. Under any circumstance where cardiac injury has occurred, a ventricular arrhythmia may potentially become a lethal ventricular event. In contrast, premature ventricular contractions can occur spontaneously in healthy people without any consequence.

The chaotic nature of excitation and inefficient ventricular contraction in pathological ventricular arrhythmias frequently compromises circulation. Even ventricular tachycardia can potentially cause shock and be lethal in its own right. However, the primary danger of ventricular tachycardia is that it will decay into ventricular fibrillation, which is incapable of sustaining life and represents the majority of sudden cardiac death cases. Thus, the indication that ventricular tachycardia or ventricular fibrillation might occur demands prompt therapeutic intervention.

There has been considerable investigation into methods of evaluating premonitory signs that might predict susceptibility to serious ventricular arrhythmias. One approach involves monitoring the heartbeat continuously for long periods of time (24 to 72 hours), with patients recording their activity in diaries during the monitoring process (called Holter monitoring). In addition to evaluating ventricular rhythm disturbances associated with serious cardiac arrhythmias, this method also allows for the identification of potential causative conditions. Patients with coronary artery disease often undergo an exercise test that examines ventricular rhythm under circumstances in which part of the heart is receiving insufficient blood. This is a useful way of predicting potential problems associated with ventricular arrhythmias in these patients.

Ventricular Fibrillation

Ventricular fibrillation is characterized by the irregular and uncoordinated contraction of the muscle fibres of the ventricles. Since ventricular fibrillation completely prevents the heart from functioning as a pump, it quickly brings death unless emergency measures restore the circulation of oxygenated blood throughout the body.

Ventricular fibrillation may result from heart attack or from electric shock, deprivation of oxygen, certain chemical imbalances in the blood (abnormally high levels of potassium or low levels of calcium), or the administration of certain drugs. Treatment centres on cardiopulmonary

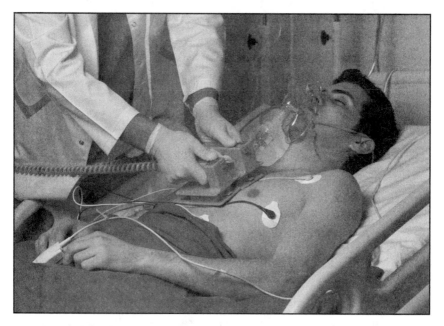

Use of defibrillators in patients experiencing cardiac arrest has greatly improved their chances of recovery since their first use in 1947. © www. istockphoto.com / Serdar Yagci

resuscitation (CPR), electrical defibrillation (the administration of electric shocks), and antiarrhythmic drugs. These measures are supplemented by closed chest massage, which serves to maintain systemic circulation and the integrity of the vascular beds.

HEART FAILURE

Heart failure is a general condition in which the heart muscle does not contract and relax effectively, thereby reducing the performance of the heart as a pump and compromising blood circulation throughout the body. Heart failure is not a specific disease but the result of many different underlying conditions, such as heart attack, hypertension (high blood pressure), cardiac valve insufficiency (leaking) or stenosis (narrowing), and exposure to toxins (alcohol or some cancer treatments).

When heart failure occurs, the ability of the heart to contract is decreased (systolic dysfunction), or the heart becomes stiff and does not relax normally (diastolic dysfunction). In some cases both conditions exist together. With less blood ejected from the heart at each beat, the body attempts to compensate for the decreased circulation to peripheral organs. Perhaps the most important response is the retention of salt and water by the kidneys in an attempt to increase intracardiac pressures and improve circulatory volume. As a result of these reflex actions, patients with heart failure usually show signs of congestion, along with weight gain and swelling of the extremities and abdominal organs—a condition known as congestive heart failure. Patients with congestion in the lungs or chest cavity suffer from short-windedness, particularly with exertion or while trying to lie flat. The heart's response to the systemic effects of circulatory failure is to enlarge the chambers (cardiomegaly) and increase the muscle mass (hypertrophy).

CONGESTIVE HEART FAILURE

Congestive heart failure is a condition resulting from a variety of cardiac diseases associated with an inadequate pumping function of the heart. The inability of the heart to pump effectively leads to accumulation of blood in the lungs and veins, reduced blood flow to tissues, and accumulation of fluid in tissues (edema), causing circulatory congestion.

Congestive heart failure results in part from the consequences of mechanisms that compensate for cardiac dysfunction and in part from direct effects of decreased blood flow to the heart. These problems are often related to salt and water retention in tissues, and the symptoms they produce can vary from minimal to pulmonary edema (abnormal accumulation of fluid in the lungs) to sudden cardiac death. Chronic states of varying severity may last years. Symptoms tend to worsen as the body's attempts to compensate for the condition create a vicious circle. The patient has trouble breathing, at first during exertion and later even at rest.

In healthy individuals, cardiac output is adjusted by a rapid increase in the strength of contraction that occurs almost immediately upon an increase in activity. After this increased contractility, additional changes in cardiac output arise from adjustment of the heart rate. For this reason, maximum cardiac output is closely linked to the maximum achievable heart rate. While improved strength and efficiency of contraction can be demonstrated in athletes, maximum achievable heart rate appears to be almost entirely a function of age. Maximum achievable heart rate begins to decline at approximately 30 years of age and gradually decreases throughout the remainder of life. The percentage maximum of cardiac work an individual patient achieves under certain workloads (i.e., during exercise testing) is a measure of how well the patient's heart is functioning. Disturbances in cardiac output may be a sign of cardiac dysfunction that can lead to congestive heart failure.

Causes of congestive heart failure include coronary artery disease, heart attack, cardiomyopathy, untreated hypertension, congenital heart defects, heart valve disease, and chronic kidney disease. However, a large group of people develop ventricular dysfunction and congestive heart failure with no obvious cause. While the incidence of heart attack, and the resulting severity of cardiac injury, has fallen, it remains one of the most common etiologies of congestive heart failure. This occurs in part because of the marked increase in survival of heart attack patients who have severely compromised hearts. Heart failure due to cardiac valve disease has decreased in the developed world because of the marked reduction in rheumatic heart disease and the improvement of cardiovascular surgical approaches. Similarly, surgical approaches to congenital heart abnormalities have reduced the incidence of congestive heart failure related to congenital syndromes.

Studies using molecular genetics techniques have demonstrated the presence of specific genetic mutations in cardiac proteins associated with cardiomyopathy clustering in families. It is not clear whether spontaneous cardiomyopathies are associated with random genetic mutations of these proteins. The etiology of congestive heart failure affects both preventative and therapeutic approaches.

VENTRICULAR DYSFUNCTION IN HEART FAILURE

The major role of the ventricles in pumping blood to the lungs and body means that even a slight decrease in ventricular efficiency can have a significant impact on heart function. If the left ventricle encounters either absolute or relative functional insufficiency (called left ventricular heart failure, or left-sided heart failure), a series of compensatory reactions are initiated that may temporarily provide a return to sufficient ventricular function. One mechanism of compensation associated with left ventricular failure is left ventricular enlargement, which can increase the volume of blood that is ejected from the ventricle, temporarily improving cardiac output. This increase in size of the ventricular cavity (called ventricular dilation), however, also results in a reduction in the percentage of the left ventricular volume of blood that is ejected (called ejection fraction) and has significant functional consequences. Ejection fraction, therefore, is a benchmark for assessing ventricular function and failure on a chronic basis.

The result of a fallen ejection fraction is an enlargement of the ventricular volume during diastole that occurs by ventricular dilation, which serves as a first-line compensatory mechanism. When this happens, the ventricle recruits additional contractile units in myocardial cells that cause the cells to stretch further than they would normally, so they can generate a stronger contraction for ejection. Dilation is necessary for the dysfunctional ventricle to maintain normal cardiac output and stroke volume (the volume of blood ejected with each contraction). This acute compensatory mechanism, called the Frank-Starling mechanism (named for German physiologist Otto Frank and British physiologist Ernest Henry Starling), may be sufficient in patients with mild heart failure who only require ventricular compensation during exercise, when demand for cardiac output is high. Increased ventricular volume, however, results in an increase in internal load. Over time the ventricle responds by increasing the size of individual muscle cells and thickening the ventricular wall (ventricular hypertrophy). Ventricular hypertrophy causes increased stiffness of the left ventricle, thereby placing a limitation on the amount of compensatory increase in ventricular volume that can be generated.

The need for increased ventricular filling in a stiff ventricle results in an increase in left ventricular filling pressure during the period of time that blood is flowing from the left atrium to the left ventricle (diastole). Atrial pressure must be increased in order to fill the ventricle, resulting in increased pulmonary venous pressure. Increased pulmonary venous pressure results in congestion (due primarily to a distended pulmonary venous population), which stiffens the lung and increases the work of breathing (dyspnea). Thus, compensation for ventricular dysfunction results in shortness of breath, particularly on exertion, which is the cardinal feature of congestive heart failure.

Other features of congestive heart failure result from a compensatory mechanism in the body to maintain stroke volume. Receptors located in the large arteries and the kidneys are sensitive to alterations in cardiac function. The latter respond by secreting an enzyme called renin that promotes sodium retention, which leads to fluid retention. Thus, a compensatory mechanism for inadequate blood circulation is expansion of the blood volume. Increased blood volume is an indication that fluid is being lost from the circulation into the extracellular fluid. Fluid accumulation in tissues (edema) accounts for several of the clinical signs of congestive heart failure. Edema is frequently seen as swelling, particularly of the lower extremities, where there is accumulation of subcutaneous fluid. When severe enough, pressure on this swelling results in a temporary crater or pit (pitting edema). Similarly, edema may occur in the pulmonary circulation (pulmonary edema). The symptoms may vary from shortness of breath on very little exertion to a medical emergency in which the patients feel as though they are suffocating. Congestive symptoms may also result in enlargement of the liver and spleen and loss of fluid into the abdominal cavity (ascites) or the pleural cavity (pleural effusion), profoundly affecting organ function and respiratory function.

In patients with less severe disease, congestive symptoms at rest are minimal because of decreased cardiac load associated with inactivity. However, if fluid overload persists, when the patient lies down and elevates dependent extremities (e.g., the legs), large amounts of fluid become mobilized, resulting in rapid expansion of the blood volume and in shortness of breath. Shortness of breath on lying down is called orthopnea and is a major symptom of heart failure. In addition, the patient may experience acute shortness of breath while sleeping (paroxysmal nocturnal dyspnea) that is related to circulatory inadequacy and fluid overload. When this occurs, the patient is awakened suddenly and suffers severe anxiety and breathlessness that may require half an hour, or longer, from which to recover.

A limited amount of heart failure is initiated in the right ventricle, though it may also be caused by cor pulmonale or disease of the tricuspid valve. Right ventricular heart failure (sometimes called right-sided heart failure) results in right-sided alterations in the pulmonary circulation. These alterations may be associated with severe lung diseases, such as chronic obstructive lung disease, and poorly understood primary diseases, such as primary pulmonary hypertension. Since the right side of the heart is the direct recipient of venous blood, the primary signs of this illness are venous congestion and enlargement of the liver.

Compensatory mechanisms also cause expansion of fluid volume and edema in the feet and legs. Pulmonary congestion does not occur in right ventricular heart failure because back pressure into the lungs is required for this condition, and the normal function of the right ventricle is to pump blood forward into the pulmonary circulation. In severe (terminal) right ventricular heart failure, cardiac output becomes significantly reduced, leading to metabolic acidosis. Historically, right ventricular heart failure was also associated with mitral valve disease and congenital heart disease, but the incidence of these two conditions has been greatly reduced as a result of surgical advancements.

TREATMENT OF HEART FAILURE

Treatment of heart failure is complex and multifaceted. Of prime importance is treatment of the specific underlying disease (such as hypertension, valvular heart disease, or coronary heart disease). For example, surgical intervention may be used to repair congenital or valvular heart defects. The primary goal of this approach is to avoid potential heart failure associated with complications of congenital or valvular defects, such as ventricular overload. Despite improved therapies for coronary artery disease and efforts to educate people about the importance of reducing risk factors for atherosclerosis, coronary artery disease remains one of the most common causes of heart failure.

Prescribed medications for heart failure are usually aimed at blocking the adverse effects of the various neurologic, hormonal, and inflammatory systems activated by heart failure. These generally include drugs such as angiotensin-converting enzyme (ACE) inhibitors and other vasodilators, which relax the smooth-muscle lining of the veins and arteries and thereby lower blood pressure and decrease the heart's workload; beta-blockers, which reduce excitatory reaction in response to sympathetic nervous system stimulation, thereby helping to stabilize the heartbeat; and aldosterone antagonists to decrease salt retention (aldosterone is a steroid hormone that regulates the balance of salt and water in the body). Diuretics are prescribed to remove excess fluid. Digoxin and digitoxin are commonly prescribed to increase the strength of heart contraction. (These latter drugs evolved from digitalis, which was introduced in the 18th century as one of the first effective remedies for congestive heart failure, known at the time as "dropsy.") Administration of these classes of agents has been shown to have considerable benefits directly related to their ability to control blood pressure.

Patients are also advised to limit their intake of salt and fluids, avoid alcohol and nicotine, optimize their body weight, and engage in aerobic exercise as much as possible. Much can be done to prevent and treat heart failure, but ultimately the prognosis depends on the underlying disease causing the difficulty as well as the severity of the condition at the time of presentation.

The treatment of heart attack has important consequences with respect to long-term mechanical function of the ventricle. In fact, congestive heart failure is the major cause of cardiac death after heart attack, often appearing within one to two years after the initial attack. Heart attack therapy is often designed to reduce the amount of damage caused by rapid revascularization immediately following the attack. The process of revascularization plays an important role in stimulating ventricular remodeling that leads to ventricular dysfunction. Improved emergency response and prevention of complications that may arise during heart attack, such as arrhythmias, have resulted in a significant reduction of cardiac deaths from heart attack. Therapies designed to promote efficient repair and scar formation in the ventricle also reduce sudden death and the incidence of heart failure.

Therapy of progressive heart failure is generally targeted toward decreasing blood volume by increasing salt and water excretion. In patients who have no symptoms at rest and only mild symptoms while exercising (sometimes called incipient heart failure), salt restriction and diuretics may be sufficient. In patients with marked restriction of exercise capacity or with symptoms at rest (mild to moderate heart failure), there is significant benefit from low doses of beta-blockers, renin-angiotensin system inhibitors, and inhibitors of aldosterone. Patients with symptoms at rest or with minimal activity (moderate to severe heart failure) have a particularly poor long-term prognosis, with approximately half of these patients dying within two years from cardiac dysfunction or rhythm disturbances. Thus, more aggressive strategies have arisen to maintain these patients and to improve their prognosis.

Heart transplants have been performed since 1967 but are much more successful today because of effective treatments that reduce immune rejection of the donor heart. However, cardiac transplant is still limited by the availability of donor hearts, and, while antirejection strategies have been generally effective, they may cause complications, such as accelerated atherosclerosis and changes in cardiac cells, that ultimately result in transplant failure. While life expectancy following a heart transplant is difficult to predict, the average recipient will live 8 to 10

Heart transplants are one way to treat congenital and acquired heart disease. Artificial implants, such as this full-implantable one presented in 2008, have been a huge step in cardiology, allowing cardiologists to treat greater numbers of patients with damaged and diseased hearts. Patrick Kovarik/AFP/ Getty Images years. This has fostered ongoing investigation into better strategies to manage immune rejection.

Because of the unpredictable nature of obtaining a donor heart, left ventricular assist devices have been developed to increase patient survival while awaiting a transplant. These devices work by taking part of the blood from the left ventricle and mechanically pumping it into the arterial circulation. This mechanical assistance reduces the amount of work required of the left ventricle. Some patients who have received left ventricular assist devices as "bridges" to transplant have actually demonstrated significant recovery of their native ventricular function. A dramatic improvement in health and quality of life in some of these patients has eliminated the need for a transplant. Long-term ventricular assist devices, for use in patients who are not candidates for heart transplant, have been approved as well.

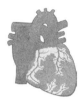

CHAPTER 6

DISEASES OF THE BLOOD VESSELS

Diseases of the blood vessels affect the ability of blood to circulate through the body and can have important consequences on heart and vascular function. These diseases often arise from abnormalities in vessel walls, with hardening of vessels being one of the most common pathologies.

Each of the different types of blood vessels can be affected by disease. Of the arteries, perhaps the most significant disease is atherosclerosis, a condition that represents a major public health problem in developed countries such as the United States. Atherosclerosis contributes to the development of other cardiovascular diseases, including heart attack and stroke.

Diseases of the veins and capillaries also can have deleterious impacts on the heart. Examples of such conditions include varicose veins and capillary hemorrhage (rupture). Because of the diverse etiology and progression of blood vessel diseases, there exist a number of different approaches to their effective diagnosis and treatment.

DISEASES OF THE ARTERIES

There are many types of arterial diseases. Some are generalized and affect arteries throughout the body, though often there is variation in the degree they are affected. Others are localized. These diseases are frequently divided into those that result in arterial occlusion (blockage) and those that are nonocclusive in their manifestations.

ATHEROSCLEROSIS

Atherosclerosis is a chronic disease caused by the deposition of fats, cholesterol, calcium, and other substances in the innermost layer of endothelium (the intima) of the large and medium-sized arteries. Atherosclerosis is the most common arterial abnormality characterized as arteriosclerosis, which is defined by the loss of arterial elasticity due to vessel thickening and stiffening.

The precise mechanisms of atherosclerosis are not completely understood, but there is evidence that in some people the condition can begin in childhood with the formation of tiny "fatty streaks," or streaks of fat deposition, in the arteries. As the endothelium is infiltrated by more and more fatty materials—primarily

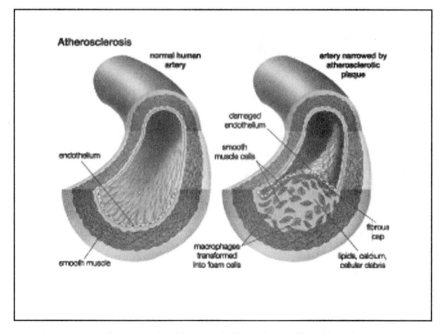

A comparison between a healthy vein (left) *and one affected by atherosclerosis* (right). Encyclopædia Britannica, Inc.

low-density lipoproteins (LDLs), protein-lipid complexes that serve as a vehicle for delivering cholesterol to the body—immune cells called macrophages are drawn to the site to scavenge the materials. When filled with lipids the macrophages become known as "foam cells." These cells grow increasingly inefficient at lipid removal and eventually undergo cell death, accumulating at the site of lipid deposition in the endothelial lining.

Other materials are also deposited in the lining, including salts of calcium and other minerals, smooth muscle cells, and cellular debris of varying composition. This causes the initially tiny lesions to enlarge and thicken to form atheromas, or atherosclerotic plaques. These plaques, which can be of variable distribution and thickness, may narrow the vessel channel, interfering with the flow of blood. Under most conditions the incorporation of LDLs is the predominant factor in determining whether or not plaques progressively develop. Endothelial injury, either as a result of lipid deposition or as a result of another cause, may also be accompanied by the formation of fibrous caps of scar tissue. These areas of scar tissue make the vessel walls less elastic, with one consequence being an increase in blood pressure. Thick plaques that severely occlude an artery can significantly decrease the flow of blood to vascular beds in tissues served by the artery, thereby causing severe tissue damage.

In addition, a disturbance to the endothelium may result in the formation of a blood clot (thrombus) at the site of a plaque, likewise obstructing the channel or breaking loose from the site and causing a catastrophic blockage elsewhere. Clot formation is directly associated with endothelial injury, since this process leads to the involvement of two cell types that circulate in the blood—platelets and monocytes (a type of white blood cell).

Platelets adhere to areas of endothelial injury and to themselves. They trap fibrinogen, a plasma protein, leading to the development of platelet-fibrinogen thrombi. Platelets deposit pro-inflammatory factors, called chemokines, on the vessel walls.

Atherosclerotic lesions frequently are found in the aorta and in large aortic branches. They are also prevalent in the coronary arteries, where the condition is called coronary heart disease (also called coronary artery disease or ischemic heart disease). The distribution of lesions is concentrated in points where arterial flow gives rise to abnormal shear stress or turbulence, such as at branch points in vessels. In general the distribution in most arteries tends to be closer to the origin of the vessel, with lesions found less frequently in more distal sites.

Hemodynamic forces are particularly important in the system of coronary arteries, where there are unique pressure relationships. The flow of blood through the coronary system into the heart muscle takes place during the phase of ventricular relaxation (diastole) and virtually not at all during the phase of ventricular contraction (systole). During systole the external pressure on coronary arterioles is such that blood cannot flow forward. The external pressure exerted by the contracting myocardium on coronary arteries also influences the distribution of atheromatous obstructive lesions.

When atherosclerosis affects the coronary arteries, which bring oxygen-rich blood to the heart muscle, it can decrease the supply of blood to the heart muscle and result in chest pain known as angina pectoris. The complete occlusion of one or more coronary arteries can cause the death of a section of the heart muscle (heart attack). Atherosclerotic lesions of the cerebral vessels may lead to formation of blood clots and stroke.

Epidemiology of Atherosclerosis

The six principal risk factors for atherosclerosis include age, genetics, gender, serum cholesterol concentrations, smoking, and diabetes. In addition, obesity and stress can place a person at greater risk of the disease.

The prevalence of atherosclerosis increases with age, and young children with evidence of fatty streaks are very likely to develop the disease when they are older. In addition, occurrence of atherosclerosis in some families is linked to a genetic component, and family history serves as a useful predictor for the course of development of the disease, particularly if it is evident at a young age. There are several important genetic defects of lipid metabolism, one of which involves a defect of lipoprotein receptors and constitutes an extreme form of familial propensity for atherosclerosis.

Men develop atherosclerosis more often than women, and complications generally appear at an earlier age. One reason for this difference has been ascribed to estrogen, a female hormone that induces high-density lipoproteins (HDL) which remove excess cholesterol from arterial cells, thus providing a protective effect against development of atherosclerosis in women. When estrogen levels decrease after menopause, the incidence of atherosclerosis and its complications rises. Though hormone replacement therapy was once considered an anti-atherosclerotic therapy for women, controversy surrounding the long-term effects of hormone therapy has greatly reduced their use for cardiovascular conditions.

Epidemiological observation has demonstrated that patients with high serum cholesterol and lipoprotein concentrations have a higher incidence of atherosclerosis. Increased cardiovascular risk lies mainly in cholesterol associated with LDL and very low-density lipoproteins

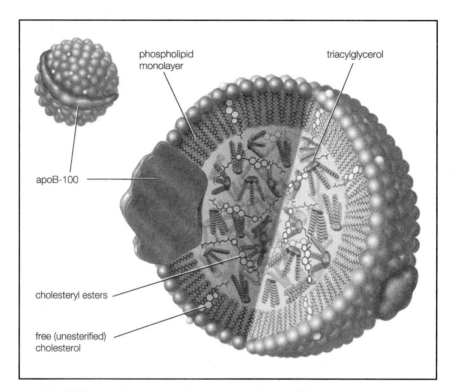

The LDL complex is essentially a droplet of triacylglycerols and cholesteryl esters encased in a sphere made up of phospholipid, free cholesterol, and protein molecules known as apoprotein B-100 (ApoB-100). The LDL complex is the principal vehicle for delivering cholesterol to body tissues through the blood. Encyclopædia Britannica, Inc.

(VLDL) that contain large amounts of cholesterol relative to HDLs and deliver cholesterol directly to the cells of peripheral tissues, including arteries. There are also some qualitative abnormalities in lipoproteins that appear to control the risk of atherosclerosis and are also associated with familial propensity.

Smoking may increase the risk of developing atherosclerosis and its associated complications, with one pack of cigarettes a day doubling the risk and two packs a day tripling it. Smoking also increases the incidence of adverse coronary events in young women taking oral contraceptives.

Complications of atherosclerosis are a significant cause of lowered life expectancy in smokers.

Incidence of atherosclerotic disease and its complications in patients with either type 1 (insulin-dependent) or type 2 (non-insulin-dependent) diabetes is significantly higher than in healthy individuals. This appears to be so even when accounting for abnormal blood lipids frequently associated with diabetes and poor diabetic control, suggesting that high blood sugar may potentially injure the artery and facilitate atherosclerosis. Patients with diabetes also frequently have high levels of triglycerides, which appear to be associated with diabetes and its complications.

In addition to these primary risk factors, there is substantial evidence that other factors such as sedentary lifestyle, environmental stress, and obesity increase risk. Atherosclerosis and its complications have also been associated with elevated levels of the blood amino acid homocysteine. However, this is unlikely to account for many cases of the disease. Great attention has been placed on the reduction of risk factors as therapeutic strategy for treatment and prevention of atherosclerosis.

Complications of Atherosclerosis

Complications of atherosclerosis constitute a major cause of death in many industrialized countries. The major complications of atherosclerosis are associated with occlusion (blockage) or inadequate blood flow to organs perfused by the affected artery. However, changes in the mechanical stability and characteristics of the artery itself may result in a series of nonocclusive complications. The aorta and the iliac arteries sometimes become mechanically unstable and dilate, forming aneurysms (widening of an artery because of the destruction of the arterial wall). These aneurysms may favour the formation of blood clots that break off and occlude vessels downstream, or they may burst and hemorrhage, which may be fatal. The aorta also loses its elasticity and may actually calcify (harden). Blood ejected into a rigid aorta encounters increased flow resistance that is manifested by increased cardiac work and elevated systolic blood pressure. These factors may be important in the development of heart failure, high blood pressure, and stroke in elderly patients.

Occlusive complications of atherosclerotic disease occur by two mechanisms that have strikingly different clinical pictures, even though both arise from the presence of atherosclerosis. Chronic occlusive disease develops over time as atherosclerotic deposition increases plaque size and tends to occlude the vessel. While this does not often occur in the aorta, chronic occlusive disease can significantly alter flow in very large aortic branches, such as the carotid and iliac arteries. Occlusions of the coronary vessels may also occur slowly over time.

Under the circumstances of chronic occlusion, there are a variety of mechanisms by which the vessel can adapt and maintain blood flow. One adaptation is through the formation of new vessels (collateral circulation). In addition, the blood vessel itself may dilate in response to increased atherosclerotic obstruction (vessel remodeling). Chronic occlusion will not alter resting blood flow until lumen occlusion becomes greater than 70 percent. Prior to this stage the reduction of blood flow in a specific vascular bed occurs, symptoms of which are first noted under conditions of stress. For example, in coronary artery disease, the patient may be asymptomatic at rest and only have pain when exercising. Exercise testing is often used to diagnose chronic stable coronary artery disease. As the vessel becomes more occluded and resting blood flow is reduced, the patient becomes more susceptible to acute complications, such as heart attack.

The atherosclerotic plaque is also susceptible to disruptive influences that may result in the formation of a blood clot (thrombus) on its surface, favouring an acute thrombotic occlusion in the vessel and acute atherosclerotic complications. Because the occlusion occurs very quickly, the body does not have an opportunity to compensate or respond to this occlusion, and, unless prompt treatment is available, distal tissues will be damaged as a result of inadequate blood flow (ischemia). When this occurs in the coronary circulation, the result is heart attack. When it occurs in the cerebral circulation, the result is stroke. Acute thromboses cause irreversible damage to tissues and are associated with loss of function of portions of organs, such as occurs in the heart following heart attack or in the brain following cerebral stroke.

Prevention of Atherosclerosis

Strategies for prevention of atherosclerosis are aimed at alteration of risk factors. Patients are urged to improve their diet and to exercise in order to lower their cholesterol and better their lipoprotein profile. If lifestyle modifications are unsuccessful, statins, drugs that act primarily by inhibiting cholesterol synthesis and also possibly by stabilizing the atherosclerotic plaque, are often prescribed to reduce the chances of a thrombotic event. Similarly, cessation of smoking is clearly a mechanism to reduce incidence of atherosclerosis.

People who have had a heart attack or stroke, or are at high risk for either, are often prescribed daily low-dose aspirin therapy. Maintaining a steady low level of aspirin in the blood prevents atherosclerotic complications by blocking the ability of platelets to stick together to form blood clots. It has also been shown that aspirin decreases the risk of death from heart attack if it is given during or immediately after the attack.

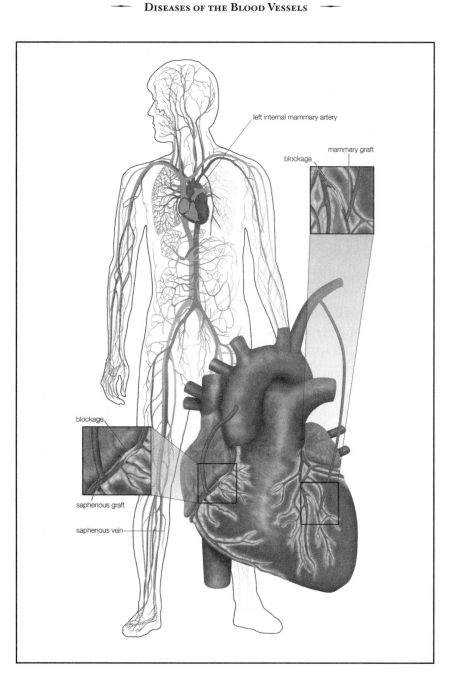

Double coronary artery bypass surgery, showing the grafting of a section of saphenous vein from the leg to bypass a blockage on the right side of the heart and the diversion of an internal mammary artery to bypass a blockage on the left side of the heart. Encyclopædia Britannica, Inc.

Treatment of Atherosclerosis

Treatment of chronic occlusive disease is aimed at opening or bypassing the occluded vessel. However, vessels can also be replaced surgically via several techniques. In the carotid circulation, atherosclerotic plaques can be directly removed from vessels to reestablish open blood flow via a procedure called atherectomy, in which a tiny knife inserted into a vessel through a catheter is used to shave fatty deposits off the vessel wall.

Occlusion of the coronary arteries is treated using coronary artery bypass surgery. This procedure relocates native vessels, such as the saphenous vein (from the leg) or the internal mammary artery (in the chest), to the heart, where they serve to bypass the flow of blood around the occlusion. Replacement of the large arteries and the aorta with Dacron™ grafts is quite common.

Noninvasive methods have been developed to open chronic atherosclerotic occlusions using a catheter in a procedure called angioplasty. In balloon angioplasty, a catheter is inserted at the site of obstruction and a balloon is inflated in order to dilate the artery and flatten the plaque deposits, essentially allowing blood to flow around the obstruction. Passages opened in this way frequently reclose over time, but the chances of this occurring can be reduced significantly by the insertion of expandable wire-mesh stents as part of the angioplasty procedure. Some stents are "drug-eluting," that is, coated with a drug that inhibits the kind of cell growth that leads to reclosure (restenosis).

Acute closure of vessels in the coronary circulation is treated in several ways. Proteolytic enzymes (enzymes that break down proteins) or drugs that activate the proteolytic process are often used for clot dissolution. The most commonly used therapeutic agent is tissue

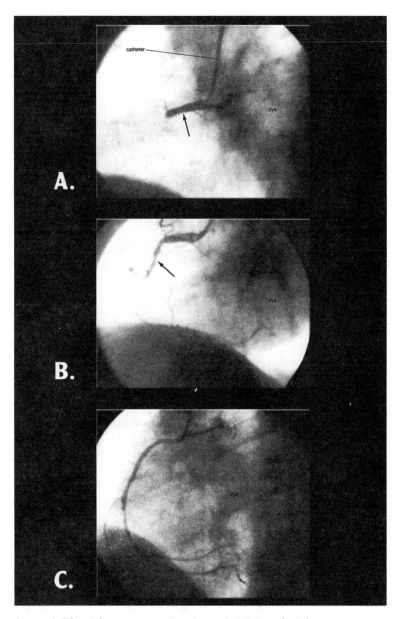

(A; top) *The right coronary artery* (arrow) *is injected with an opaque contrast medium through a catheter in the aorta. The artery is completely blocked by a thrombus (blood clot) 1 cm (0.4 inch) from its origin.* (B; middle) *The same right coronary artery* (arrow) *30 minutes after the start of intravenous thrombolytic treatment; the clot is beginning to dissolve.* (C; bottom) *The right coronary artery completely unblocked.*

plasminogen activator (t-PA), which is given intravenously and acts rapidly to dissolve clots. Acute coronary thrombosis can also be treated by angioplasty, almost always accompanied by insertion of a stent and resulting in rapid and complete restoration of blood flow. However, since the blood clotting mechanism is compromised by the use of thrombolytic agents, such as t-PA, there is a substantial incidence of bleeding during and following stent implantation that can be fatal. This complication has led to a relative reluctance to utilize these procedures in older patients because of the possibility of producing hemorrhagic stroke. Regardless of the method, time is a critical factor in the success of restoring proper blood flow, and early recognition of symptoms has become a major health education goal.

In patients at risk for thrombotic events, antiplatelet or anticoagulant drugs can be used to decrease platelet aggregation and to prevent the formation of thrombi. Statins, which have been shown to reduce the level of cholesterol and fat in the blood, can also reduce the incidence of acute arterial events through an anti-inflammatory mechanism, although how this occurs is not fully understood. Other drugs such as aspirin, which prevents the formation of blood clots, may be effective in avoiding a thrombotic event. In addition, several dietary habits have been associated with lower incidence of acute thrombotic events, including high intake of vitamin E and fish oil and drinking red wine. However, extensive studies are needed to confirm these effects.

THROMBOSIS

The formation of a blood clot in the heart or in a blood vessel is known as thrombosis. Factors that play a role in the formation of clots (thrombi) include injury to a blood vessel and alterations from normal blood flow. Changes in the coagulability of the blood may also cause clot formation. Injury to the lining of a blood vessel or of the heart that results, for example, from inflammation or from atherosclerosis may lead to clot formation.

Normally the formed elements of the blood—the red and white blood cells and the platelets—move along in the centre of the stream in a blood vessel. If there is turbulence or other alteration from normal flow, the platelets and blood cells may scrape along the blood vessel lining. Such a situation may arise at the site of an aneurysm. Confinement in bed also may result in more sluggish blood flow in the veins and consequent formation of a clot. Abnormally large numbers of platelets may cause an increased tendency of the blood to coagulate, as may abnormally high levels of fats in the blood.

Effects of thrombosis may be blockage of the blood vessel at the point of clot formation or blockage of a vessel at some other point by a clot that has broken free from its point of origin. Such a clot is called an embolus.

EMBOLISM

Embolism occurs when there is an obstruction in the flow of blood caused by an embolus, a particle or aggregate of substance that is abnormally present in the bloodstream. The substance may be a blood clot that has broken loose from its point of formation (while it is still adherent to the vessel at the point where it was formed, it is called a thrombus). For example, emboli may originate from blood clots formed in the chambers of a diseased or abnormally functioning heart. Mural thrombosis on the infarcted ventricular wall or clots in the atrium in atrial fibrillation are common sources of emboli.

An embolus can occur in the form of a variety of other substances. For example, it may be a drop of soluble fat from a crushing injury of fatty tissue (e.g., fat emboli may occur after a fracture of bone and the discharge of fatty marrow), or it may be a clump of tumour cells, bacteria, or detached tissue cells. Bacterial emboli occur in bacterial endocarditis and occasionally in other infections. Cancers may produce minute emboli of tumour cells. Fungus growth or foreign materials, such as fragments of bullets, may become emboli. These emboli may cause transient local symptoms from diminished blood flow and may result in death of tissue. Treatment may include anticoagulant therapy and surgical removal of the clot.

Other sources of emboli include foreign bodies, such as a bullet that has penetrated a vessel wall, amniotic fluid that has entered the maternal circulation during childbirth, or an air bubble (called an air embolism) or a bubble of some other gas — for example, nitrogen in decompression sickness. Air emboli may be suspected after major injury, especially when large veins are opened during accidents or during vascular surgery of the neck or chest cavity.

So long as the embolus travels unimpeded through the bloodstream, it is not likely to cause symptoms or damage. However, if the substance blocks a vessel that supplies blood to the brain, a stroke may occur, with effects that include a period of unconsciousness, temporary or lasting paralysis of all or part of one side of the body, inability to use words (aphasia), impaired memory, and, in severe cases, death. Embolism in a coronary artery, which supplies blood to the heart muscle, can cause a number of serious effects, including death of a section of the heart muscle (heart attack).

A pulmonary embolism — an obstruction of blood flow to the lungs by an embolus in the pulmonary artery or in one of its branches — results in difficulty in breathing and an unpleasant sensation beneath the breastbone, similar to that experienced in angina pectoris. Pulmonary embolism may occur in an apparently healthy individual. If the embolus is small, it may not have any effect on the systemic circulation. With larger pulmonary emboli, there may be massive bleeding from the lungs and the development of a large area of pulmonary infarction, resulting in sudden death.

Treatment of embolism varies with the cause and site of the embolus, although anticoagulant drugs are generally administered to help prevent recurrence due to blood clot formation. Getting up and walking soon after an operation or after congestive heart failure is the best method for avoiding pulmonary embolism. Anticoagulant therapy is useful both as prevention and as therapy after the condition has developed. Surgical removal of a massive pulmonary clot has, on rare occasions, been spectacularly successful.

STROKE

Stroke, or apoplexy, is a sudden impairment of brain function resulting either from a substantial reduction in blood flow to some part of the brain or from intracranial bleeding. The consequences of stroke may include transient or lasting paralysis on one or both sides of the body, difficulties in speaking or eating, and a loss in muscular coordination. A stroke may cause cerebral infarctions—dead sections of brain tissue.

Risk Factors for Stroke

Aging is one of the greatest risk factors for stroke, with the risk increasing significantly after age 55. Other major risk factors include hypertension, smoking, high cholesterol, diabetes, and heritable defects. In addition, stroke is more common in men than in women, and the risk of death from stroke is higher in African Americans than in Caucasians. This difference is primarily due to the higher prevalence of hypertension in African Americans.

Some people are predisposed to stroke because of genetic factors. Scientists have identified genetic variations that increase the risk of stroke. In a study involving almost 20,000 people in Europe and the United States, one specific variation was found to occur in 10 percent of African Americans and 20 percent of Caucasians. This particular variation, known as a single nucleotide polymorphism (SNP), occurs on chromosome 12 and is closely associated with ischemic stroke, which arises due to an insufficient supply of blood to the brain. Although the mechanism by which this SNP contributes to stroke is not known, knowledge of such variants can lead to the development of improved diagnostic techniques and new treatments.

Causes of Stroke

The most common cause of stroke is a blood clot that has formed within a blood vessel of the brain. A blood clot also can lodge in an artery supplying brain tissue after originating in another portion of the body and traveling to the brain (embolism). A heart attack, damage to a heart valve, and an irregular heartbeat called atrial fibrillation can cause blood clots that may reach the brain. Both types of clots reduce or stop the flow of blood to brain cells. During the early stages of stroke from a blood clot, the condition may be further complicated by the leakage of blood and fluid into the surrounding areas (edema).

Stroke can also occur as a result of atherosclerosis, the buildup of fatty deposits on artery walls. Atherosclerosis can cause intermittent insufficiency in the flow of blood due to spasm of the arteries, which can rupture, or the sludging of the blood as it passes through segments of vessels that have been narrowed by fatty deposits.

Types and Symptoms of Stroke

A hemorrhagic stroke, involving intracranial bleeding, may occur after an artery ruptures, usually as a result of a weakening of the arterial wall because of atherosclerosis or because of a thinning of the wall along with bulging (aneurysm), often due to hypertension.

Transient ischemic attacks, or ministrokes, result when long, thin arteries penetrating deep into the brain become blocked by atherosclerosis, causing areas of surrounding tissue to lose their blood supply. The tissue may then wither, creating minute holes, called lacunes. A succession of transient ischemic attacks over the years can riddle the brain, causing dementia.

The initial onset of stroke may be massive in its effects, producing widespread paralysis, inability to speak, coma, or death within a short time, usually within several hours or days. On the other hand, the onset may be manifested by a series of transient ischemic attacks during which the patient may experience weakness and numbness of an arm, a leg, or a side of the face. There may be temporary difficulty in speech, confusion, or visual disturbances. Transient ischemic attacks may recur many times, but they are usually followed eventually by more widespread and permanent paralysis.

The groups of muscles and nerves involved are a direct reflection of the artery and brain tissues involved. If the left side of the brain (the dominant side for most persons) is affected, there is a paralysis of the right side of the body because most of the nerves cross to the opposite side of the body from their origin in the brain. However, the combinations of signs and symptoms are innumerable.

Diagnosis and Treatment of Stroke

Precise history and physical examination, especially for neurological changes, are essential to differentiate stroke from a tumour and from brain injury resulting from other causes. It is also important to determine whether the stroke is due to a thrombus, embolism, or hemorrhage. Examination of the spinal fluid for evidence of blood is often essential. Diagnostic imaging (as by computerized tomography [CT] scan) may clarify the diagnosis. Establishing a differential diagnosis is essential because anticoagulant drugs are widely used in the treatment of stroke due to thromboses or emboli but are contraindicated when due to hemorrhage. A stroke may have both a clotting and a significant hemorrhagic factor present, and this presents difficulties. Many strokes are due to closure of one of the two carotid arteries that supply the brain after passing up the sides of the neck from the aorta. If the closure involves only a small segment, surgery may be attempted to remove the obstruction or to insert a graft or synthetic bypass.

Many persons who have a stroke live for years after the event. Early and persistent efforts for rehabilitation are essential, including both physical, occupational, and speech therapy. These therapies should begin within a day or two after the stroke.

ARTERITIS

Arteritis is the inflammation of an artery or arteries, occurring primarily within localized segments of the vessels. Arteritis may occur in a number of diseases, including syphilis, tuberculosis, pancreatic disease, serum sickness (a reaction against a foreign protein), and lupus erythematosus (a systemic disease that has also been attributed to some form of immune reaction).

Temporal, or cranial, arteritis (also known as giant-cell arteritis), which involves inflammation of the temporal arteries and of other arteries in the cranial area, is of unknown cause, although it is usually preceded by an infection. It is a disease of variable duration. It may persist for as long as three years or may subside in a few months. Most persons affected are women in their 50s or older. The disease usually starts with a headache, which may be accompanied by fever and by pain in the scalp, face, jaws, and eyes. The affected person may find it difficult to move her jaws because of deficiency of blood flow to the jaw muscles. Paralysis of the eye muscles — ophthalmoplegia — may cause the affected person to see double, a condition called diplopia. Fluid may collect in the retina and in the optic disk, the point at which the optic nerve enters the eyeball. This condition leads to vision loss in about 50 percent of those diagnosed. The chief danger of temporal arteritis is its effect upon the eyes. Excision of the involved artery may be carried out, but the general symptoms may remain.

Takayasu arteritis (pulseless disease) is a rare form of arteritis that affects the aorta and its branches. The disease frequently is found in people of Asian ancestry, and it is more common in women than men. Inflammation of the arteries eventually may block the supply of blood to the head, neck, the arms, and part of the body wall, which can result in blindness and paralysis. Most deaths from the disease result from damage to the heart muscle and to the brain.

Polyarteritis nodosa, or periarteritis nodosa, is another type of arteritis and is characterized by inflammation of the arteries and surrounding tissue. It may affect functioning of adjacent organs. The cause of polyarteritis nodosa is unknown, although hypersensitivity may play an important role. The word *nodosa* ("knotty") forms part of the name because of the fibrous nodules along the medium-sized arteries that are affected. Men are more susceptible than women.

The effects of polyarteritis nodosa appear to occur as a result of occlusion or bleeding or a combination of the two. The course of the disease varies. It may be rapid, involving only weeks or months, or it may be highly prolonged. The involvement of the blood vessels may affect blood flow to the skin, the gastrointestinal tract, the kidneys, and the heart. There may be associated symptoms of arthritis, and involvement of almost all organs has been noted. There is an associated fever in most instances, an increase in the number of leukocytes in the blood, and evidence of inflammation. The condition is diagnosed by microscopic examination of inflamed tissue.

Although no recognized specific mode of therapy is available for the various forms of arteritis, patients have responded to a number of anti-inflammatory therapies (such as glucocorticoids) and immunosuppressant drugs.

ARTERIOVENOUS FISTULA

An arteriovenous fistula is an abnormal direct opening between an artery and a vein. It may be congenital in origin. It also may result from vascular disease, from complications of surgery, or from accidental penetration wounds. In fact, arteriovenous fistulas are common injuries of war, frequently resulting from the penetration of shell fragments and other types of injury involving the arms and legs.

An arteriovenous fistula allows large amounts of blood to be shunted from the artery to the vein. The arterial blood is passed to the venous side of the fistula, and the blood pressure in the vein increases, causing distension. Symptoms include an aching pain in or beyond the area of the injury and puffy legs that frequently show distended veins. When there is an arteriovenous fistula, the pulse in the vein is diminished by direct compression of the supplying artery, resulting in a continuous murmur that may help in diagnosing and locating the fistula. Normal blood flow can usually be reestablished by surgery.

The physician may hear a loud murmur caused by the turbulent flow of blood from the artery to the vein. Enlargement of the heart and all the manifestations of congestive heart failure may occur if the amount of blood shunted is large. In the area around the site of the arteriovenous fistula, the blood vessels become dilated and bacterial infection of the artery lining may develop. A cure can usually be achieved by surgery, though in some situations the remaining arterial flow may be impaired.

A special kind of arteriovenous fistula occurs from the pulmonary artery to the pulmonary vein. There the situation is complicated by the fact that unoxygenated venous blood is being shunted into a vessel normally containing oxygenated blood. Cyanosis results and produces a stimulation for the formation of red blood cells, leading to a form of secondary polycythemia, or abnormally high red-blood-cell level.

RAYNAUD SYNDROME

Raynaud syndrome is said to occur when the extremities— including occasionally even the ears, nose, or cheeks—become pale, cyanotic, and numb under the influence of cold or emotion. Pain is also present at times. On cessation of the stimulus, redness develops, and there is a tingling or burning sensation lasting some minutes.

This sequence of events is apparently caused by the excessive constriction of the small arteries and arterioles of the fingers upon stimuli that ordinarily cause only a minor degree of vasoconstriction. Raynaud syndrome, which is initially manifested by this phenomenon, involves spasmodic contraction of the blood vessels, usually beginning in early adulthood and affecting women about three times as often as men. The limb involvement is usually symmetrical (on both sides) and may lead to gangrene. Attacks may subside after the return to a warm environment or the release from tension.

The symptoms associated with Raynaud syndrome may occur in people without other evidence of organic disease, especially in cold and moist climates. It may result from the operation of pneumatic hammers or may occur in individuals with various disorders, such as a cervical rib, a supernumerary (extra) rib arising from a neck vertebra. It may appear as a complication of arteriosclerosis and thromboangiitis obliterans. Various substances, such as nicotine, arsenic, ergot, and lead, have occasionally been blamed. Therapy includes treatment of the primary condition and avoidance of the precipitating cause.

ACROCYANOSIS

Acrocyanosis is a bluish discoloration of the hands caused by spasms in arterioles (small arteries) of the skin. It is similar to Raynaud syndrome in that it is characterized by episodes of coldness and cyanosis of the hands and feet. It is often associated with profuse sweating of the fingers and toes and, at times, with local edema.

Although it is understood that acrocyanosis represents a form of local sensitivity to cold, the underlying cause of the condition is unknown. It is most common in women, particularly in adolescents and those in their 20s.

It is also frequently seen in mentally or emotionally disturbed people or in those with neurocirculatory asthenia (a symptom-complex in which there is breathlessness, giddiness, a sense of fatigue, pain in the chest over the heart, palpitation, and a fast and forcible heartbeat of which the affected person is conscious). Reassurance and avoidance of cold help to eliminate attacks. The condition usually improves with age.

ERYTHROMELALGIA

Erythromelalgia (sometimes called erythermalgia) is a rare disease in which the blood vessels of the hands and feet go through spasms of dilation associated with burning pain, increased skin temperature, and redness. It especially affects the palms of the hands and the soles of the feet, which may be hot and are often somewhat swollen. Dilation of the blood vessels (vasodilation) is the underlying factor.

Erythromelalgia usually occurs in middle and later life. The disease may be primary, in which case the cause is unknown and tends to be chronic. Secondary erythromelalgia is caused by underlying disorders of the nervous system or blood (vascular) system. For example, it may occur as a manifestation of an abnormally high red-blood-cell level or as the result of injury or a variety of other disorders.

Erythromelalgia may be exacerbated by external heat and exercise. Treatment includes rest, elevation of the extremity, and cold applications. Aspirin can be used to relieve pain.

AORTIC ARCH SYNDROME

Aortic arch syndrome refers to a group of disorders that cause blockage of the vessels that branch off from the aorta in the area in which the aorta arches over the heart. The aorta is the principal vessel through which the heart pumps oxygen-rich blood into the systemic circulation. The aortic branches that may be affected supply blood to the head, the neck, the arms, and part of the body wall. Most often the condition occurs in middle-aged or elderly persons and is caused by atherosclerosis, in which fatty plaques form in the artery lining.

A rare form of the aortic arch syndrome that primarily affects Asian women is the previously mentioned Takayasu disease, or nonspecific arteritis. The progressive blockage causes impaired cerebral circulation, which can lead to blindness and paralysis. Most deaths from the disease result from damage to the heart muscle and to the brain. Treatment involves bypass grafting.

Congenital defects of the aortic arch include persistent ductus arteriosus, in which the channel connecting the aorta and the pulmonary artery in the fetus does not close after birth and must be closed surgically, and coarctation (narrowing) of the aorta, which causes an increased workload on the left ventricle.

OTHER INJURIES TO ARTERIES

Arteries also are susceptible to physical injuries arising from various causes. Physical injuries to arteries may lead to damage of the vascular wall, with consequent formation of blood clots and blockage. On other occasions, a form of inflammation can develop that may lead to rupture and may be the source of emboli in the peripheral arteries. Sudden disastrous external stress—as in a severe automobile accident, airplane crash, or underwater explosion—may cause death through rupture of the major arteries, such as the aorta, rupture of the heart valves, or rupture of the heart itself.

X-rays, radium, and other radioactive substances in large dosages have marked effects on the vascular system. Initial reactions are inflammatory, and secondary changes caused by scarring and retractions may occur, which in turn lead to vascular occlusion (obstruction). The effects may be progressive for a period of years and are, at times, complicated by the development of cancer.

DISEASES OF THE VEINS

In general, diseases of the veins are characterized by inflammation or vessel distension. There are several important conditions affecting veins. Examples include thrombophlebitis, varicose veins, and hemorrhoids. These diseases range from being relatively benign, having little or no impact on overall cardiovascular heath, to severe, giving rise to potentially dangerous adverse events such as embolism.

THROMBOPHLEBITIS

Inflammation of a vein coupled with formation of a blood clot (thrombus) that adheres to the wall of the vessel is known as thrombophlebitis. The inflammation may precede or follow formation of the clot. In the latter case, the presence of a clot within a vein can give rise to variable amounts of inflammatory reaction in the vessel wall. As a result, in some instances, the inflammatory reaction is predominant and thrombosis is secondary, whereas in other instances, thrombosis appears before reaction in the vein wall. Embolization—breaking loose of a blood clot— is most likely to occur during this period, though it may occur at any stage of the disease.

Thrombophlebitis most frequently involves the veins of the legs. It may occur without apparent cause and tends to recur. At times it occurs as a result of local injury, either from a penetrating wound or from an external blow without a break in the skin. It may occur as a result of severe muscular effort or strain and in the course of infectious diseases, thromboangiitis obliterans, and a wide range of other underlying diseases. Thrombophlebitis may develop in various parts of the body if there is cancer, especially cancer of the pancreas. The presence of varicose veins in the legs causes a tendency to the development of thrombophlebitis.

There may be pain at the site of the blockage or throbbing pain throughout the leg. If the affected vein is near the surface, it feels like a cord to the touch. Because movement of the blood through veins depends upon contractions of the muscles, prolonged inactivity (such as bed rest after a surgical procedure or during convalescence from a serious illness) may lead to insufficient movement of the blood through the veins, with resultant formation of clots and inflammation. Pulmonary embolism may occur in bedridden persons as a result of a clot from a thrombophlebitic lesion

Treatment of thrombophlebitis is primarily by administration of anticoagulant or fibrinolytic drugs, slight elevation of the affected leg, application of heat, elastic supports, and brief periods of walking to encourage circulation. Occasionally surgical treatment may be necessary. A form of the disease in which little or no inflammatory reaction or pain develops is called phlebothrombosis.

VARICOSE VEINS

A varicose vein, or varix, is a twisted vein that has become distended with blood. The term *varix* is also used for similar abnormalities in arteries and in lymphatic vessels. Varicose veins occur in a number of areas, including the legs, the esophagus, the spermatic veins (which return blood from the testes; varicose veins in this area cause a mass in the scrotum that is called a varicocele), around the rectum or anus (hemorrhoids), the veins of the broad ligaments (i.e., folds of peritoneal membrane) that extend from the uterus to the walls of the pelvis, and the veins of the urinary bladder.

Varicose veins are permanently twisted and enlarged. The condition may occur without obvious cause or as a result of postural changes, occupation, congenital anomaly, or localized causes of increased venous pressure. The veins may be near the surface and easily seen, or they may be hidden and unrecognized. Without complication they rarely cause symptoms, but they may become the site of thrombophlebitis with inflammatory changes and the production of emboli in the peripheral circulation.

Varicose veins in the legs, by far the most common location, result from malfunctioning of the valves in the veins. These valves normally prevent blood from reversing its flow after the movement of the leg muscles has forced the blood upward and from superficial veins to the deep veins. When the valves do not function properly, the blood collects in the superficial veins, distending and twisting them. Weakness of the valves and of the walls of the veins may be inherited. Hormones also play a role in the development of varicose veins, which explains the increase in the number of varices that occurs during pregnancy and menopause.

The veins may rupture on occasion, with bleeding into the surrounding tissues. In all forms of varicose veins, the walls of the veins become hardened, and a certain amount of inflammation develops through the years. Dilated veins in the legs may be supported by appropriate elastic-type stockings or bandages, or they may be treated by surgery.

Symptoms include a sensation of heaviness and a tendency for the leg muscles to cramp while one is standing.

The feet and legs swell at the end of the day. The skin may be inflamed and moist, a condition called weeping eczema. Ulcers may appear around the ankles, and clots may develop in the diseased blood vessels (thrombophlebitis).

Treatment consists of the use of elastic bandages or strong support hose; sclerotherapy, which involves the injection of a solution that closes the vein, causing blood to be rerouted to healthier veins; and surgical treatment, which may consist of removing the affected veins (e.g., vein stripping) or closing the veins endoscopically or with the use of lasers.

HEMORRHOIDS

Hemorrhoids, or piles, are masses formed by distension of the network of veins under the mucous membrane that lines the anal channel or under the skin lining the external portion of the anus. A form of varicose vein, a hemorrhoid may develop from anal infection or from increase in intra-abdominal pressure, such as occurs during pregnancy, while lifting a heavy object, or while straining at stool. It may be a complication of chronic liver disease or tumours. The weakness in the vessel wall that permits the defect to develop may be inherited.

Mild hemorrhoids may be treated by such methods as the use of suppositories, non-irritating laxatives, and baths. If clots have formed, or have formed in the presence of other complications, the hemorrhoids may be removed surgically.

VENOSPASM

Direct mechanical injury or an infection or other disease process in the neighbouring tissues may produce spasms in the veins (venospasms). Local venospasm is usually of relatively minor significance because of the adequacy of alternate pathways for the blood. If venospasm is widespread, however, involving an entire extremity or the veins in the lungs, it may impair blood flow and therefore be of greater significance.

DISEASES OF THE CAPILLARIES

The capillaries are the smallest blood vessels. Through their thin walls oxygen and nutrients pass to the tissue cells, in exchange for carbon dioxide and other products of cellular activity. Despite the small size and thin walls of the capillaries, the blood pressures may be quite high, as, for instance, in the legs of a person in a motionless upright position. In certain disease states there is increased fragility of the capillary wall, with resultant hemorrhages into the tissues. These hemorrhages are referred to as petechiae when small. If large, they may become a large area of discoloration of the skin. Vitamin C deficiency and a variety of blood disorders may be associated with increased capillary fragility. Small petechial hemorrhages occur in bacterial endocarditis and certain other infectious processes. In some instances petechiae are caused by minute emboli. In others they appear to be directly related to capillary fragility itself. Treatment is of the underlying disorder.

The capillaries are freely permeable to water and small molecules but ordinarily are not highly permeable to proteins and other materials. In some pathological situations, such as in certain allergic states (e.g., hives) or because of local injury, as in burns, there may be local areas of permeability, with escape of fluid high in protein into the surrounding tissues. If the disease affects the entire body, a significant amount of plasma (the blood minus its cells) leaks into the nonvascular spaces, with resultant loss in blood volume. Again, treatment is of the underlying disorder.

ANGIOMA

A congenital mass of blood vessels that intrudes into bone or other tissues, causing tissue death and, in the case of bone, structural weakening, is known as an angioma. Angiomas of the bone are often associated with angiomas of the skin or muscles. Most angiomas remain asymptomatic, but they may cause collapse of the vertebrae if they occur in the spine, and hemorrhage is a danger in some locations that expose them to stress. Treatment is usually by radiation, which causes clot formation within the mass of vascular tissue. The clot will then gradually calcify. Surgery also may be performed but involves a risk of hemorrhage.

CHAPTER 7

HEMODYNAMIC DISORDERS AND SHOCK

H emodynamic disorders and shock arise from abnormalities in the forces driving the circulation of blood through the body. Often these disorders are associated with the physical mechanisms controlling the movement of the blood and especially with factors involved in the maintenance of blood pressure.

Disorders of blood flow are often characterized by either increased or decreased pressure of the blood as it circulates through the body. When blood is forced through the vessels at a pressure higher than normal, the fragile tissues that make up the walls of blood vessels are at risk of damage. In contrast, when blood circulates with less pressure than normal, syncope (fainting) and shock may result.

HEMODYNAMIC DISORDERS

The two primary types of hemodynamic disorders are hypertension, or high blood pressure, and hypotension, or low blood pressure. These conditions differ from the normal rise and fall of blood pressure that are associated with everyday activities, such as exercise and sleep. Hypertension and hypotension are associated with disease processes, and in many cases involving hypertension, the resulting increase in blood pressure can cause long-term damage to the cardiovascular system and to organs throughout the body.

HYPERTENSION

Hypertension occurs when the body's smaller blood vessels (the arterioles) narrow, causing the blood to exert excessive pressure against the vessel walls and forcing the heart to work harder to maintain the pressure. Although the heart and blood vessels can tolerate increased blood pressure for months and even years, eventually the heart may enlarge (a condition called hypertrophy) and be weakened to the point of failure. Injury to blood vessels in the kidneys, brain, and eyes also may occur.

Blood pressure is actually a measure of two pressures, the systolic and the diastolic. The systolic pressure (the higher pressure and the first number recorded) is the force that blood exerts on the artery walls as the heart contracts to pump the blood to the peripheral organs and tissues. The diastolic pressure (the lower pressure and the second number recorded) is residual pressure exerted on the

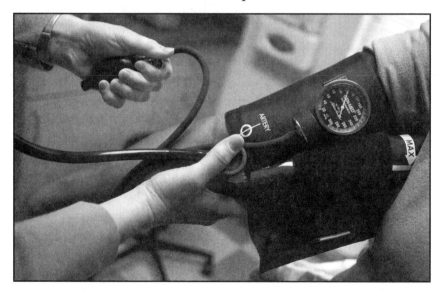

Here a patient has her blood pressure checked by a doctor. Regular checks of blood pressure help doctors ensure that a patient's heart is healthy. Joe Raedle/ Getty Images

arteries as the heart relaxes between beats. A diagnosis of hypertension is made when blood pressure reaches or exceeds 140/90 mmHg (read as "140 over 90 millimetres of mercury").

When there is no demonstrable underlying cause of hypertension, the condition is classified as essential hypertension. (Essential hypertension is also called primary or idiopathic hypertension.) This is by far the most common type of high blood pressure, occurring in up to 90 percent of patients. Genetic factors appear to play a major role in the occurrence of essential hypertension. Secondary hypertension is associated with an underlying disease, which may be renal, neurologic, or endocrine in origin. Examples of such diseases include Bright disease (glomerulonephritis; inflammation of the urine-producing structures in the kidney), atherosclerosis of blood vessels in the brain, and Cushing syndrome (hyperactivity of the adrenal glands). In certain structural abnormalities of the aorta, such as coarctation, in which the artery's middle coat is deformed with resultant narrowing of the channel, arterial pressure in the upper half of the body is abnormally high. In cases of secondary hypertension, correction of the underlying cause may cure the hypertension.

Various external agents also can raise blood pressure. For example, excessive dietary intake of salt has long been held to be responsible for hypertension in certain people. Stress has also been shown to cause hypertension, and fear and anxiety can induce a rise in blood pressure owing to increased activity in the sympathetic nervous system. Hormones and other vasoactive substances, including cocaine, amphetamines, cold remedies, thyroid supplements, corticosteroids, nonsteroidal anti-inflammatory drugs (NSAIDs), and oral contraceptives, have a direct effect on blood pressure, but the interaction of these factors remains unclear.

Malignant hypertension is present when there is a sustained or sudden rise in diastolic blood pressure exceeding 120 mmHg, with accompanying evidence of damage to organs such as the eyes, brain, heart, and kidneys. Malignant hypertension is a medical emergency and requires immediate therapy and hospitalization.

Elevated arterial pressure is one of the most important public health problems in developed countries. In the United States, for instance, it is generally accepted that 15 to 20 percent of the adult population is hypertensive and often undiagnosed. High blood pressure is significantly more prevalent and serious among African Americans. Age, race, sex, smoking, alcohol intake, elevated serum cholesterol, salt intake, glucose intolerance, obesity, and stress all may contribute to the degree and prognosis of this disease. In both men and women, the risk of developing high blood pressure increases with age. Until age 55 more men than women have hypertension. After that the ratio reverses. Hypertension has been called the "silent killer" because it usually produces no symptoms. It is important, therefore, for anyone with risk factors to have their blood pressure checked regularly and to make appropriate lifestyle changes.

People with hypertensive disease have an increased susceptibility to atherosclerosis of the coronary arteries, thus making it difficult to separate the cardiac manifestations from those actually caused by hypertension. Hypertensive people, therefore, may eventually have congestive heart failure following enlargement of the heart caused by the chronic increase in arterial pressure. In addition, they may suffer the effects of a decline in blood supply to the heart because of coronary artery disease and the classic manifestations of coronary arteriosclerosis, such as angina pectoris or heart attack. Hypertensive cardiovascular disease may also become manifest through defects in the vessels supplying the brain, leading to stroke. Furthermore, hypertensive cardiovascular manifestations may be complicated by the development of kidney failure and the resultant abnormal retention of fluid in the tissues, adding to the problems of congestive heart failure.

Effective treatment will reduce overall cardiovascular morbidity and mortality. Nondrug therapy consists of: (1) relief of stress; (2) dietary management (restricted intake of salt, calories, cholesterol, and saturated fats; sufficient intake of potassium, magnesium, calcium, and vitamin C); (3) regular aerobic exercise; (4) weight reduction; (5) smoking cessation; and (6) reduced intake of alcohol and caffeine.

Before the use of antihypertensive drugs, high blood pressure was associated with a greatly increased mortality, with survival measured in months in the most severe cases. Thus, antihypertensive drugs have dramatically increased the life expectancy of patients with severe hypertension. Mild to moderate hypertension may be controlled by a single-drug regimen, although more severe cases often require a combination of two or more drugs.

Diuretics are a common medication. These agents lower blood pressure primarily by reducing body fluids and thereby reducing peripheral resistance to blood flow. However, they deplete the body's supply of potassium, so it is recommended that potassium supplements be added or that potassium-sparing diuretics be used. Beta-blockers inhibit the effects of epinephrine (adrenaline), thus easing the heart's pumping action and widening blood vessels. Vasodilators act by relaxing smooth muscle in the walls of blood vessels, allowing small arteries to dilate and thereby decreasing total peripheral resistance. Calcium channel blockers promote peripheral vasodilation and reduce vascular resistance. The angiotensin-converting enzyme (ACE) inhibitors inhibit the generation of a potent vasoconstriction agent (angiotensin II), and they also may retard the degradation of a potent vasodilator (brady-kinin) and involve the synthesis of vasodilatory prostaglandins. Angiotensin receptor antagonists are similar to ACE inhibitors in utility and tolerability, but instead of blocking the production of angiotensin II, they completely inhibit its binding to the angiotensin II receptor. Statins, best known for their use as cholesterol-lowering agents, have shown promise as antihypertensive drugs because of their ability to lower both diastolic and systolic blood pressure. The mechanism by which statins act to reduce blood pressure is unknown. However, scientists suspect that these drugs activate substances involved in vasodilation.

HYPOTENSION

Hypotension is abnormally low blood pressure caused either by reduced blood volume or by increased blood-vessel capacity. Though not in itself an indication of ill health, it often accompanies disease.

Extensive bleeding is an obvious cause of reduced blood volume that leads to hypotension. There are other possible causes. A person who has suffered an extensive burn loses blood plasma—blood minus the red and white blood cells and the platelets. Blood volume is reduced in a number of conditions involving loss of salt and water from the tissues—as in excessive sweating and diarrhea—and its replacement with water from the blood. Loss of water from the blood to the tissues may result from exposure to cold temperatures. Also, a person who remains standing for as long as one-half hour may temporarily lose as much as 15 percent of the blood water into the tissues of the legs.

Orthostatic hypotension—low blood pressure upon standing up—seems to stem from a failure in the autonomic nervous system. Normally, when a person stands up, there is a reflex constriction of the small arteries and veins to offset the effects of gravity. Hypotension from an increase in the capacity of the blood vessels is a factor in fainting. Hypotension is also a factor in poliomyelitis and in overdose of depressant drugs, such as barbiturates.

Hypotension may occur in persons who are weak and enfeebled but more often does not represent a diseased state. Hypotension of a severe degree may develop in heart failure, after hemorrhage, in overwhelming infections, and in a variety of circumstances that lead to the development of the clinical picture of shock. In shock the circulation is inadequate, blood pressure is low, heart rate is rapid, and irreversible tissue damage from insufficient blood supply may occur if the condition is not terminated.

BAINBRIDGE REFLEX

The Bainbridge reflex, or atrial reflex, is an acceleration of the heart rate resulting from increased blood pressure in, or increased distension of, the large systemic veins and the right upper chamber of the heart. This reflex, first described by the British physiologist Francis Arthur Bainbridge in 1915, is a normal response and prevents the pooling of blood in the venous system.

Special pressure sensors called baroreceptors (or veno-atrial stretch receptors) located in the right atrium of the heart detect increases in the volume and pressure of blood returned to the heart. These receptors transmit informa-tion along the vagus nerve (10th cranial nerve) to the central nervous system. This response results in the acti-vation of sympathetic nerve pathways that serve to increase the strength of contraction of the heart muscle and to increase heart rate (tachycardia). The Bainbridge reflex can be blocked by atropine, is diminished or absent when the initial heart rate is high, and can be abolished by cutting the vagus nerves.

Syncope

Syncope is an effect of temporary impairment of blood circulation to a part of the body. The term is most often used as a synonym for fainting, which is caused by insufficient blood flow to the brain as a result of a fall in blood pressure. Syncope is characterized by the sudden loss of consciousness associated with a transient disorganization of circulatory function, as differentiated from other brief losses of consciousness associated with abnormal central nervous system activities, as in certain forms of epilepsy. Syncope involving temporary unconsciousness may also be caused by any of a number of organic (physical) diseases or disorders, such as aortic stenosis, heart failure, and a low level of sugar in the blood.

The most common kind of syncope is ordinary fainting. Some individuals are more susceptible than others. Blood loss, exhaustion, the presence of other illness, and psychological factors may contribute to a tendency to faint. Fainting tends to be preceded first by paleness, nausea, and sweating and then by dilatation of the pupils, yawning, and deeper and more rapid breathing. The heart rate at this time is usually relatively rapid, but, with the abrupt onset of syncope, the heart rate often falls to below the normal level, and the person collapses as if dead. The faint usually lasts from a fraction of a minute to several minutes and may be followed by headache, confusion, nervousness, and a feeling of weakness. There is usually a rapid recovery without complications.

Carotid sinus syncope, sometimes called the tight-collar syndrome, also causes brief unconsciousness from impaired blood flow to the brain. Unlike the ordinary faint, this syncope is not preceded by pallor, nausea, and sweating. (The carotid sinus is a widened portion of the carotid artery where there are nerve endings sensitive to pressure. When they are stimulated, the heart is slowed, blood vessels dilate, and blood pressure consequently falls, causing, in turn, reduction in blood flow to the brain.) Pressure on the carotid sinuses by a tight collar, by turning the head to the side, in swallowing, or even in shaving the side of the neck over the carotid sinus may be sufficient to cause the syncope, or it may occur spontaneously. This syncope may be used diagnostically, since faintness upon massage of one carotid sinus may suggest a narrowed carotid or basilar artery on the opposite side of the neck.

Local syncope is whitening, weakness, coldness, and numbness of a small area of the body, especially the fingers, as a result of diminished blood flow to the part. It is associated with Raynaud syndrome.

Syncope can occur with any cardiac rhythm disturbance that compromises circulation, such as a transient cessation of circulatory activity due to heart block. Other forms of syncope occur as a result of lowered blood pressure upon assumption of an upright position, a condition often called orthostatic hypotension. In some individuals, disease of the autonomic nervous system prevents appropriate postural adjustments for the upright stance. The disorder may be caused by vascular or central nervous system involvement of the autonomic system. In other instances, postural hypotension may occur as a result of inadequate blood volume, of taking various drugs that affect the nervous control of the circulation, and from a wide variety of other causes. Transient hypotension also may result from hypersensitivity of the carotid sinus. Patients with stenotic (narrowed) aortic or mitral valves may experience syncope during exercise. These patients are at high risk for sudden cardiac death.

PHYSIOLOGICAL SHOCK

Physiological shock may be defined as acute progressive circulatory failure, in which the tissues receive an inadequate supply of blood and its components (such as nutrients and oxygen) and an inadequate removal of wastes. The result is cell damage and, eventually, cell death. This definition is derived from the one constant feature of physiological shock: the failure of adequate blood flow through the capillaries, the smallest of the blood vessels. Shock may be so severe as to impair organ function or create a state of blood flow deficiency that grows progressively more dangerous.

Shock is usually caused by hemorrhage or overwhelming infection and is characterized in most cases by a weak, rapid pulse; low blood pressure; and cold, sweaty skin. Depending on the cause, however, some or all of these symptoms may be missing in individual cases. Shock may result from a variety of physiological mechanisms, including sudden reductions in the total blood volume through acute blood losses, as in severe hemorrhage; sudden reductions in cardiac output, as in heart attack; and widespread dilation of the blood vessels, as in some forms of infection. Whatever the central physiological mechanism, the effect of shock is to reduce blood flow through the small vessels, or capillaries, where oxygen and nutrients pass into the tissues and wastes are collected for removal.

Shock is usually classified on the basis of its presumed cause, although in many cases the true cause of the peripheral circulatory insufficiency may not be apparent. The most common cause of shock is massive loss of blood, either through trauma or through surgery. In the latter case, the blood loss can be anticipated and shock prevented by providing blood transfusions during and after the operation. An acute loss of blood reduces the amount of venous blood returning to the heart, in turn reducing the cardiac output and causing a drop in arterial blood pressure. Pressure receptors, or baroreceptors, in the walls of the aorta and carotid arteries trigger physiological reflexes to protect the central circulation, increasing heart rate to boost cardiac output and constricting small blood vessels to direct blood flow to essential organs. If the blood losses continue, even these mechanisms fail, producing a sharp drop in blood pressure and overt manifestations of shock. Loss of blood plasma in burns or dehydration can also lower blood volume sufficiently to induce shock.

The heart's output can also be reduced sufficiently to produce shock without blood loss. In coronary thrombosis, the supply of blood to the heart muscle through the coronary artery is interrupted by a blood clot or vascular constriction. The damaged muscle may then lack strength to force a normal volume out of the heart with each stroke. Again, the diminished output triggers the baroreceptors in the arteries to restrict peripheral circulation. Blood clots that block the circulation of blood to the lungs (pulmonary emboli) or increase the fluid that surrounds and cushions the heart (cardiac tamponade) can also impair the pumping of the heart sufficiently to cause shock.

The most common cause of shock by dilation of the blood vessels is massive bacterial infection, which may be further exacerbated by reductions in total blood volume caused by fluid losses secondary to the infection. Generally, toxins produced by the bacteria are the cause of the dilation. Foreign substances in the bloodstream can also produce a form of shock, called anaphylactic shock, through allergic reactions causing blood vessels to dilate. Another possible cause of shock through vascular dilation is drugs. Many anesthetic drugs create a controlled shock that must be carefully monitored by adjusting dosage, and overdoses of several such drugs, including barbiturates and narcotics, produce shock symptoms.

The chief problem in treating shock is to recognize the cause of the physiological problem, as several possible causes may coexist in a single patient, especially following an accident. Failure to distinguish between shock caused by inadequate cardiac output and that caused by fluid losses reducing blood volume can result in a therapeutic dilemma, since treatments that are effective for one kind of shock will aggravate the other. Intravenous fluids are the usual treatment for shock caused by loss of blood, but adding extra fluid to the circulation can overload a damaged heart that already has a reduced output, so that the shock deepens. When the cause of shock is unclear, physicians may make a trial using intravenous fluids. If the central venous pressure rises, indicating diminished cardiac capacity, the fluids are stopped before the heart can be further compromised. Shock secondary to bacterial infection may be treated by combined fluid replacement and appropriate antibiotics, while anaphylactic shock is combated with epinephrine and antihistamines, which counter the acute allergic response.

Shock Due to Inadequate Blood Volume

Hemorrhage is the most common cause of shock. In the "average American man" (weighing 86 kg, or about 190 pounds) the blood volume is about 78 ml per kilogram (about 6.7 litres [7 quarts] for a man weighing 86 kg), and the loss of any part of this will initiate certain cardiovascular reflexes. Hemorrhage results in a diminished return of venous blood to the heart, the output of which therefore falls, causing a lowering of the arterial blood pressure. When this occurs, pressure receptors (baroreceptors) in the aorta and carotid arteries will initiate remedial reflexes either through the autonomic (non-voluntary) nervous system by direct neural transmission or by epinephrine (adrenaline) secretion into the blood from the adrenal gland.

The reflexes consist of an increase in the rate and power of the heartbeat, increasing its output; a constriction of arterioles leading to nonessential capillary beds (notably the skin and some viscera); and a constriction of the veins, diminishing the large proportion of the blood volume normally contained therein. By these means arterial blood pressure will tend to be maintained, thus preserving blood flow to the vital areas, such as the brain and the myocardium. After continued acute blood loss of 20 to 30 percent of the blood volume, the compensatory mechanism will begin to fail, the blood pressure will begin to fall, and shock will ensue.

Increased sympathetic (autonomic) nervous activity thus accounts for the fast pulse rate, pallor, and coldness of the skin in shock and, in addition, is the cause of increased sweating and dilation of the pupils of the eyes. Air hunger and mental confusion are caused by the inadequate carriage of oxygen, and decreased urine flow stems from a decrease in the renal (kidney) blood flow, which, if severe, can lead to kidney failure. If acute blood loss continues beyond about 50 percent, the inadequacy of flow through vital circulations will lead to death. Loss of whole blood is not necessary for the blood volume to be low. Plasma loss through burnt areas of the skin, dehydration following inadequate intake of fluid, or exceptional fluid loss can lead to contraction of the blood volume to levels capable of causing shock.

When it is possible to anticipate blood loss and to measure it accurately—e.g., during an operation—losses may be immediately replaced before significant volume depletion can occur. More often, however, hemorrhage is unexpected; it may not be possible to measure the amount of blood lost. If shock occurs in an otherwise healthy person, the lost blood generally is replaced by transfusion into a vein. But, since a preliminary matching between recipient serum and donor cells must be carried out and cannot be done in less than 20 minutes, other fluid is usually given intravenously during the delay. This fluid, such as plasma or a solution of the carbohydrate dextran, must contain molecules large enough so that they do not diffuse through the vessel walls. Since the main loss from burns is plasma and electrolytes, these require replacement in proportion to the area of the burn and the size of the patient.

Shock Due to Inadequate Cardiac Output

Sudden interference with the blood supply to the heart muscle, as by a thrombosis in a coronary artery, causes damage to the muscle with resultant diminution in its contractile force. The output of the heart falls. If the decline is severe, a fall in blood pressure stimulates the baroreceptors and cardiogenic shock results. This occurs uncommonly after heart attack.

But low heart output alone may not account for the shock, for in chronic heart failure the cardiac output may be low without such a response in the peripheral circulation. If widespread dilation of the veins or of the capillary beds occurs, the blood volume is no longer sufficient to fill the larger space and shock ensues.

Bacteremic Shock

Infection anywhere in the body may spread to the circulation, and the presence of organisms in the bloodstream—bacteremia—may lead to shock. Bacteria are conveniently divided into "gram-positive" and

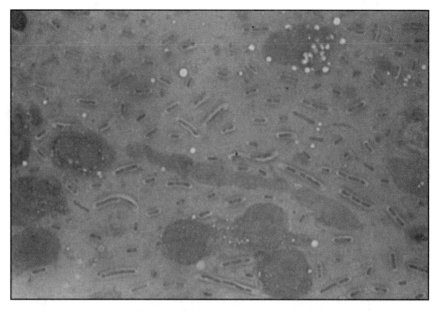

Gram-negative bacilli, Klebsiella pneumoniae, *isolated from a lung abscess in a patient with pneumonia.* A.W. Rakosy/EB Inc.

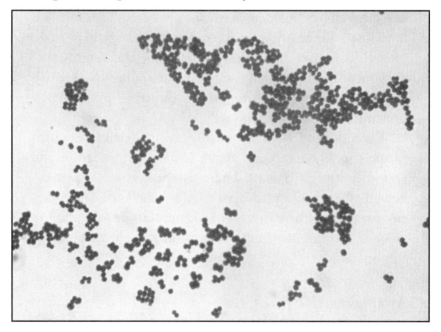

Gram-positive cocci, Staphylococcus aureus, *in a laboratory culture.* A.W. Rakosy/EB Inc.

"gram-negative" groups according to their reaction to a special staining method called the Gram stain.

Gram-negative bacteremia is the more common and more lethal type of bacteremic shock. It is frequently caused by *Escherichia coli*, *Proteus*, *Pseudomonas*, or *Klebsiella* organisms. The first of these normally inhabits the intestine. The clinical picture of gram-negative bacteremia is much like that of hemorrhage, although no blood has been lost. This type of shock typically causes a rapid, thready pulse; cold, sweaty skin; and low blood pressure. A fever may occur, in addition to the local signs of the associated infection. The cause of the type of reaction is uncertain. The response to bacteremia from gram-positive organisms such as *Staphylococcus* and *Streptococcus* is different: widespread dilation of the blood vessels results in warm, dry skin and a full-volume pulse in spite of lowered blood pressure.

In both types of bacteremia the condition may be exacerbated by contraction in blood volume. This follows fluid loss—for example in the peritoneal cavity in peritonitis (inflammation of the peritoneum, the membrane that lines the abdominal cavity), in the tissues in streptococcal infection, or through the intestine in enteritis (inflammation of the intestine).

Exceeded in frequency only by cardiogenic and hemorrhagic shock, bacteremic shock is most often caused by gram-negative organisms. There are three aspects of treatment: collections of pus are drained as soon as possible; the circulatory volume is increased to compensate for enlargement of the vascular bed; and appropriate antibiotics are administered.

ANAPHYLACTIC SHOCK

An anaphylactic reaction is the direct result of the entrance of a specific foreign material into the bloodstream of a person whose body has become sensitized against it as a result of previous exposure and subsequent formation of antibodies. During an anaphylactic reaction, lung bronchi constrict intensely, narrowing the airways and interfering seriously with respiration. Blood pressure may fall precipitously because of the release of substances (serotonin, histamine, and bradykinin) that cause dilation of the arterioles and venules and an increase in the capillary wall permeability. Thus, the circulatory capacity is increased, and fluid is lost into the tissues.

The essence of treatment of anaphylactic shock is the injection of epinephrine—a powerful stimulatory drug also found naturally in the body, whose effects include an increase in the heart rate and constriction of the blood vessels—followed by an antihistamine to counteract the reaction to the foreign substance and a bronchodilator to ease breathing.

PSYCHOGENIC SHOCK

Psychogenic shock causes fainting, probably by initiating dilation of the blood vessels that perfuse the muscles. In this type of shock, blood pressure falls, the skin becomes cold and sweaty, and the pulse rate increases. A decrease in the amount of blood that is supplied to the brain leads to light-headedness and loss of consciousness. A person who is suffering from psychogenic shock should be placed flat or even with the head slightly lower than the rest of the body in order to restore a good flow of blood to the brain and to bring about recovery from the fainting.

DRUGS AND SHOCK

Most anesthetic drugs—nitrous oxide is a notable exception—have a profound effect on the circulation.

They are able to decrease the contractility of the heart muscle as well as increase the circulatory capacity by dilating the blood vessels. In addition, the normal postural circulatory reflexes are lost, so pooling of blood in the legs is liable to occur if the affected person is tilted to a head-up position. This is of particular importance after surgery. If a person is made to sit up too soon, it can lead to low blood pressure and an insufficient flow of blood to the brain. Overdosage of certain drugs—notably barbiturates, narcotics, and tranquilizers—blocks normal circulatory reflexes and causes dilation of the blood vessels, leading to a fall in blood pressure that often is accompanied by a slow, full-volume pulse.

A blood pressure that is dangerously low may be raised to safer levels by affecting the activity of the offending drug in one of many different ways. A therapeutic approach might entail, for instance, decreasing the dosage of the drug (such as an anesthetic agent), speeding up its elimination from the body, or administering a substance that is able to constrict the blood vessels. The choice of approach depends on the individual circumstance.

NEUROGENIC SHOCK

The maintenance of the tone of the blood vessels by the autonomic nervous system may be affected by severance of one of these nerves or by its interruption of the flow of nervous impulses. Thus, spinal anesthesia—injection of an anesthetic into the space surrounding the spinal cord—or severance of the spinal cord results in a fall in blood pressure because of dilation of the blood vessels in the lower portion of the body and a resultant diminution of venous return to the heart.

Neurogenic shock does not usually require specific therapy. Indeed, spinal anesthetics may be given with a view to producing a low blood pressure so as to diminish bleeding during an operation. If blood pressure becomes critically low, the legs are sometimes elevated and a vasoconstrictor administered.

ENDOCRINE CAUSES OF SHOCK

The endocrine glands play a vital role in the regulation of normal metabolic processes through the actions of their hormones. It is not surprising, therefore, that a malfunction in an endocrine gland or in its hormones has an effect on circulation. Inadequate secretion by the adrenal cortex, the outer substance of the adrenal gland, leads to shock both by the diminution of myocardial efficiency and by a decrease in the blood volume. Functional disorders of the pituitary, the adrenal medulla (the inner substance of the adrenal gland), the thyroid, and the parathyroids can all lead to circulatory upset and shock.

REFRACTORY AND IRREVERSIBLE SHOCK

The terms *refractory shock* and *irreversible shock* are widely used by physicians and other medical workers to refer to types of shock that present particularly difficult problems. The term *refractory shock* is applied when, in spite of apparently adequate therapy, the shock state continues. Commonly, the treatment later proves to have been inadequate, in which case the shock was not true refractory shock. This often occurs following a major injury in which there is internal bleeding, leading to underestimation of true blood loss and therefore to inadequate transfusion. In certain cases, however, even if the therapy actually is appropriate, the shock state persists. If patients in such cases respond to further special treatment, then this is true physiological refractory shock.

In severe or prolonged shock states, the myocardial blood supply is sufficiently diminished to damage the heart's pumping action temporarily or permanently. Also, noxious products of inadequately perfused tissues may circulate and affect the heart muscle.

While the flow of blood through major vessels is under the control of the nerves, circulation through the capillary beds is of a more primitive type and is under the influence of local metabolic products. In shock, arteriolar constriction causes inadequate flow through the tissues, and local waste products increase. These cause dilation of the capillary sphincters and opening of the whole capillary bed, which thus contains an increased proportion of the blood volume. The capillaries become further engorged with slowly flowing blood, and fluid leaks through the vessel walls into the tissues. Thus, the body is further deprived of circulating blood volume.

Widespread clotting of the blood can occur during capillary stagnation. This leads to severe damage to the cells unsupplied by flowing blood. Later, when enzymes dissolve the fibrin of the clots, the flow through these areas carries toxic metabolic products to vital organs— such as the heart, kidneys, or liver—and the ensuing damage leads to irreversibility of shock.

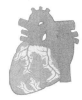

CHAPTER 8

APPROACHES TO CARDIOVASCULAR EVALUATION AND TREATMENT

The study of heart structure, function, and disease is known as cardiology. The foundation of the field was laid in 1628, when English physician William Harvey published his observations on the anatomy and physiology of the heart and circulation. At that time, the evaluation and treatment of cardiovascular diseases was based on the art of identifying a disease from its signs and symptoms. The diagnostic tests and tools available to assist physicians were few. The lungs and heart were examined primarily by applying the ear to the chest wall.

In 1816 French physician René-Théophile-Hyacinthe Laënnec invented the stethoscope, an instrument that greatly improved the ability to diagnose diseases of the heart and lungs. Laënnec's stethoscope consisted of a wooden cylinder and was monoaural, transmitting sound to only one ear. Despite the simplicity of this device, it represented a major advance in the diagnosis of respiratory and cardiovascular diseases. It enabled physicians to listen to the beating heart and to detect abnormal heart and chest sounds indicative of disease. At the end of the 19th century, Laënnec's wooden stethoscope was replaced by models using rubber tubing. Later, binaural stethoscopes, which transmit sound to both ears, came into use. Rubber binaural devices are widely used today, playing a fundamental role in the routine examination of heart.

In the 20th century a number of technological developments contributed to further improvements in cardiovascular medicine, so that today there exists a great variety of tools supported by a wide breadth of knowledge to aid physicians in the diagnosis and treatment of cardiovascular disorders. In modern medicine, the evaluation and treatment of cardiovascular diseases can be divided into noninvasive, invasive, and surgical procedures. Noninvasive procedures include evaluative techniques that are external to the body, such as electrocardiography and echocardiography. In contrast, invasive procedures involve techniques such as cardiac catheterization in which a device is inserted into the blood vessels to assess or treat cardiovascular disease. Examples of surgical procedures include open-heart surgery and coronary artery bypass, which are used to treat conditions that cannot be corrected solely through the use of pharmacological agents.

MODERN DEVELOPMENTS IN CARDIOLOGY

The modern science of cardiology deals primarily with the diagnosis and treatment of diseases and abnormalities involving the heart and blood vessels. Cardiology is a medical, not surgical, discipline. Cardiologists provide the continuing care of patients with cardiovascular disease, performing basic studies of heart function and supervising all aspects of therapy, including the administration of drugs to modify heart functions.

Much of the progress in cardiology during the 20th century was made possible by improved diagnostic tools. Electrocardiography, the measurement of electrical activity in the heart, evolved from research by Dutch physiologist Willem Einthoven in 1903, and radiological evaluation of the heart grew out of German physicist Wilhelm Conrad Röntgen's experiments with X-rays in 1895.

Echocardiography, the generation of images of the heart by directing ultrasound waves through the chest wall, was introduced in the early 1950s. Cardiac catheterization, which was invented in 1929 by German surgeon Werner Forssmann and refined soon after by American physiologists André Cournand and Dickinson Richards, opened the way for measuring pressure inside the heart, studying both

Willem Einthoven won the Nobel Prize in Physiology in 1924 for his invention of the string galvanometer, which made possible the first useful and accurate electrocardiogram (ECG). Hulton Archive/Getty Images

normal and abnormal electrical activity, and directly visualizing the heart chambers and blood vessels (angiography). In addition to these advances, the development of various imaging technologies, such as radionuclide imaging and positron emission tomography (PET), significantly advanced the detection of defects in the structure and function of heart and blood vessels.

New cardiovascular treatments also emerged in the 20th century. Drugs were developed by the pharmaceutical industry to treat heart failure, angina pectoris, coronary heart disease, hypertension (high blood pressure), arrhythmia, and infections such as endocarditis. Drug development was accompanied by the invention of procedures such as cardiac catheterization and coronary artery bypass, and open-heart surgery revolutionized the treatment of cardiovascular disease. These advances have enabled many people to survive far longer with diseased hearts than ever before in the history of medicine. In addition, the ability of emergency personnel, as well as ordinary citizens, to revive persons using techniques such as CPR (cardiopulmonary resuscitation) and defibrillation has prevented the deaths of countless people from cardiac arrest. It is expected that discoveries in genetics and molecular biology will further aid cardiologists in their understanding of cardiovascular disease.

NONINVASIVE EVALUATION TECHNIQUES

Noninvasive cardiovascular evaluation, which does not involve the introduction of devices such as probes into a patient's body, is used to obtain information about the function and structure of the heart and blood vessels. The information collected using these techniques can be used for diagnostic purposes. Some of these approaches are also employed as follow-up procedures for the examination of patients with established disease, for example, to evaluate an individual's response to certain treatments or to assess disease progression.

ECHOCARDIOGRAPHY

Echocardiography is a diagnostic technique that uses ultrasound (high-frequency sound waves) to produce an image of the internal structures of the heart. A piezoelectric transducer placed on the surface of the chest emits a short burst of ultrasound waves and then measures the reflection, or echo, of the sound as it bounces back from cardiac structures such as the heart valves and the muscle wall. The transducer does this by converting electrical impulses into a narrow ultrasonic beam that penetrates body tissues. The reflected sound waves are detected by a receiver that is also placed on the chest. The waves are transformed back into electrical impulses and are projected on the screen of a cathode-ray oscilloscope.

The reflected sound waves indicate places where changes in tissue density occur. As a result, echoes from varied depths produce an image of the walls and valves of the heart and of their motions. Such information is used to evaluate chamber size, wall thickness, and valve structure. The procedure can aid in diagnosing valve disease (e.g., endocarditis and mitral valve prolapse), congenital heart diseases, intracardiac tumours, and other cardiac abnormalities.

There are different types of echocardiography. M-mode echocardiography records the amplitude and the rate of motion of moving objects, such as valves, along a single line with great accuracy. M-mode echocardiography, however, does not permit effective evaluation of the shape of cardiac structures, nor does it depict lateral motion (i.e., motion perpendicular to the ultrasonic beam). Real-time (cross-sectional or two-dimensional) echocardiography depicts cardiac shape and lateral movement not available in M-mode echocardiography by moving the ultrasonic beam very rapidly, and such recording may be displayed on film or videotape. New techniques allow measurement by ultrasonography of rates of flow and pressures, for example, across heart valves.

BALLISTOCARDIOGRAPHY

Ballistocardiography is a graphic recording of the stroke volume of the heart for the purpose of calculating cardiac output. The heartbeat results in motion of the body, which in turn causes movements in a suspended supporting structure, usually a special table or bed on which the subject is lying, and these movements are recorded photographically (ballistocardiogram, or BCG) as a series of waves. The BCG is one of the most sensitive measures of the force of the heartbeat, and an abnormality appearing in the BCG of an apparently healthy subject aged 40, or younger, may be suggestive of symptomatic coronary disease.

RADIONUCLIDE IMAGING

Radionuclide imaging (radioactive nuclides) provides a safe, quantitative evaluation of cardiac function and a direct measurement of myocardial blood flow and myocardial metabolism. Radionuclide imaging is used to evaluate the temporal progress of cardiac disease, hemodynamics, and the extent of myocardial damage during and after infarction and to detect pulmonary infarction following emboli. The primary requirement of radionuclide imaging is that the bolus of radionuclide should remain within the blood vessels during its first passage through the right and left sides of the heart. The second requirement is that the physical properties of the radionuclide be satisfactory with respect to the instrumentation being used.

The radionuclide used in virtually all phases of radionuclide imaging is technetium-99. It has the disadvantage of a long half-life (six hours), however, and other radionuclides with shorter half-lives are also used. These radionuclides all emit gamma rays, and a scintillation camera is used to detect gamma-ray emission. The data are assessed with the R wave of the electrocardiogram as a time marker for the cardiac cycle. Radionuclide cineangiography is a further development of radionuclide imaging.

These techniques are used to assess myocardial damage, left ventricular function, valve regurgitation, and, with the use of radionuclide potassium analogues, myocardial perfusion.

There are techniques that measure metabolism in the myocardium using the radiotracer method (i.e., a radioactive isotope replaces a stable element in a compound, which is then followed as it is distributed through the body). Examples of such techniques include positron emission tomography (PET) and magnetic resonance imaging (MRI; also called nuclear magnetic resonance [NMR]).

Positron Emission Tomography

PET is an imaging technique used in the diagnosis of disease and in biomedical research. It has proved particularly useful for studying brain and heart functions and certain biochemical processes involving these organs (e.g., glucose metabolism and oxygen uptake).

In PET a chemical compound labeled with a short-lived positron-emitting radionuclide of carbon, oxygen, nitrogen, or fluorine is injected into the body. The activity of such a radiopharmaceutical is quantitatively measured throughout the target organs by means of photomultiplier-scintillator detectors. As the radionuclide decays, positrons are annihilated by electrons, giving rise to gamma rays that are detected simultaneously by the photomultiplier-scintillator combinations positioned on opposite sides of the patient. The data from the detectors are analyzed, integrated, and reconstructed by means of a computer to produce images of the organs being scanned.

PET has become a valuable tool in the detection of cancer and cancer metastasis (spread) and in the evaluation of heart conditions. PET studies have helped scientists understand more about how drugs affect the brain and what happens during learning, when using language, and in certain brain disorders, such as stroke, depression, and Parkinson's disease.

In addition, because positron radionuclides can be incorporated into true metabolic substrates, they are highly useful in biochemical research that attempts to chart the course of selected metabolic pathways, such as myocardial glucose uptake and fatty-acid metabolism. Scientists also are working to find ways to use PET to identify the biochemical nature of neurological disorders and mental disorders and to determine how well therapy is working in patients. PET has revealed marked changes in the depressed brain, and knowing the location of these changes helps researchers understand the causes of depression and monitor the effectiveness of specific treatments.

SPECT

Single photon emission computed tomography, or SPECT, is an imaging technique used in biomedical research and in the diagnosis of cardiovascular disease.

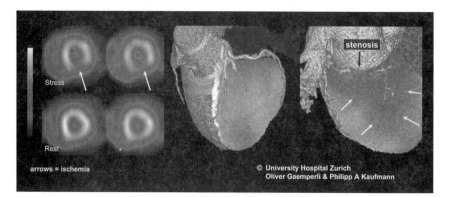

Single photon emission computed tomography (SPECT) can be used to image blood flow to the heart (left) *in order to monitor conditions such as ischemia (decreased blood flow). When information gathered via SPECT is combined with imaging information from computed tomography (CT), a fusion image* (centre and right) *can be obtained.* University Hospital Zurich

SPECT is similar to PET, in that a compound labeled with a positron-emitting radionuclide is injected into the body. However, its pictures are not as detailed as those produced using PET.

SPECT is much less expensive than PET because the tracers it uses have a longer half-life and do not require an accelerator nearby to produce them. It can be used to diagnose or evaluate a wide range of conditions, including diseases of the heart, cancer, and injuries to the brain.

Myocardial Perfusion Imaging

Myocardial perfusion imaging is a medical procedure that uses radioactive tracers, primarily thallium, to detect abnormalities in the blood supply to the heart muscle. Myocardial perfusion imaging is used to diagnose myocardial ischemia, which is caused by a reduced supply of blood to the heart; heart attack, which is an interruption of blood flow to an area of the heart; and coronary heart disease, which is an inadequate supply of blood to the heart due to the narrowing of a coronary artery.

Injected intravenously, the radioactive tracer is rapidly absorbed by the myocardium, the middle layer of muscle tissue that forms most of the wall of the heart. The tracer is normally distributed evenly in heart muscle. Thus, deficient blood flow to a portion of the myocardium is readily detectable by decreased uptake in that area. Evidence of recent and not-so-recent myocardial infarcts will be visible, but most persons with coronary heart disease who have not had a previous infarction will have normal perfusion patterns when they are at rest. In such a patient a thallium stress test is performed. The substance is injected while the individual is exercising so that areas of transient ischemia (temporary reduction in blood flow to the heart) can be identified and the patient treated to prevent heart attack. An alternative means of stressing the heart that can provide information comparable to exercise is the injection of adenosine, a vasodilator. This test is used to diagnose coronary heart disease when the resting electrocardiogram is abnormal or the exercise electrocardiogram is equivocal.

Another method for evaluating the heart without the stress of exercise involves the intravenous injection of the drug dobutamine while monitoring the effects via echocardiography. By using dobutamine echocardiography, the heart condition of frail patients and those who have heart disease or physical limitations that preclude exercise can be evaluated. Dobutamine induces the same changes in the heart that would occur during a standard exercise test. Two-dimensional echocardiography shows areas of the left ventricle that function abnormally. This technique uses no X-ray or radioactive material and is useful in diagnosing heart disease during pregnancy.

ELECTROCARDIOGRAPHY

Electrocardiography is a method of graphic tracing (electrocardiogram; ECG or EKG) of the electric current generated by the heart muscle during a heartbeat. The tracing is recorded with an electrocardiograph (actually a relatively simple string galvanometer), and it provides information on the condition and performance of the heart. The Dutch physiologist Willem Einthoven developed the first electrocardiograph in 1903, and for many years the tracing was called an EKG after the German *Elektrokardiogramm*. During the late 1960s, computerized ECGs came into use in many of the larger hospitals.

Electrocardiograms are made by applying electrodes to various parts of the body. Electrodes that record the electrical activity of the heart are placed at 10 different locations: one on each of the four limbs and six at

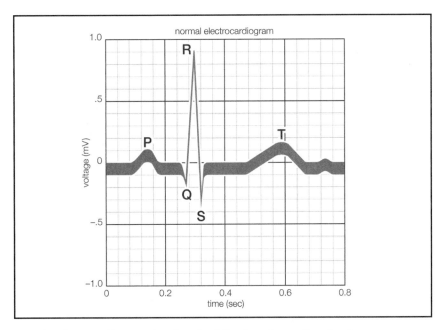

*An electrocardiogram showing the deflections that reflect the alternate con-
tractions of the atria and the ventricles of the heart during one heartbeat.*
Encyclopædia Britannica, Inc.

different locations on the anterior surface of the chest.
After the electrodes are in place, held with a salt paste,
a millivolt from a source outside the body is introduced
so that the instrument can be calibrated. Standardizing
electrocardiograms makes it possible to compare them as
taken from person to person and from time to time from
the same person.

The normal electrocardiogram shows typical upward
and downward deflections that reflect the alternate contraction of the atria (the two upper chambers) and of the
ventricles (the two lower chambers) of the heart. The first
upward deflection, P, is due to atrial contraction and is
known as the atrial complex. The other deflections—
Q, R, S, and T—are all due to the action of the ventricles
and are known as the ventricular complexes. Any

deviation from the norm in a particular electrocardiogram is indicative of a possible heart disorder.

The ECG is of greatest use in diagnosing cardiac arrhythmias, acute and prior heart attacks, pericardial disease, and cardiac enlargement (atrial and ventricular). The presence of hypertension (high blood pressure), thyroid disease, and certain types of malnutrition also may be revealed by an electrocardiogram. In addition, ECG can be used to determine whether a slow heart rate is physiological or is caused by heart block. The exercise electrocardiogram, or ECG stress test, is used to assess the ability of the coronary arteries to deliver oxygen while the heart is undergoing strain imposed by a standardized exercise protocol. If the blood supply to the heart is jeopardized during exercise, the inadequate oxygenation of the heart muscle is recorded by typical changes in the electrocardiogram that indicate coronary heart disease. However, a normal ECG does not exclude significant coronary heart disease and is not predictive of disease course.

PHONOCARDIOGRAPHY

Phonocardiography is a diagnostic technique that creates a graphic record, or phonocardiogram, of the sounds and murmurs produced by the contracting heart, including its valves and associated great vessels. The phonocardiogram is obtained either with a chest microphone or with a miniature sensor in the tip of a small tubular instrument that is introduced via the blood vessels into one of the heart chambers. The phonocardiogram usually supplements the information obtained by listening to body sounds with a stethoscope (auscultation) and is of special diagnostic value when performed simultaneously with measurement of the electrical properties of the heart (electrocardiography) and pulse rate.

CARDIAC MAGNETIC RESONANCE IMAGING

Cardiac magnetic resonance imaging (CMR; also called cardiac MRI, or heart MRI) is a three-dimensional diagnostic imaging technique used to visualize the heart and its blood vessels without the need for X-rays or other forms of radiation. Cardiac MRI employs a steady magnetic field, a radio-frequency transmission system, and computer technology to generate detailed pictures and brief videos of the beating heart. The images produced provide valuable information about heart structure and function. Cardiac MRI is used to diagnose a variety of heart conditions, including coronary heart disease, congenital heart defects, pericarditis, cardiomyopathies, heart valve disease, aneurysm, arrhythmias, and cardiac tumours.

Cardiac MRI is performed with the patient lying on his or her back on an imaging table. Electrodes are placed on the patient's chest to monitor heart rhythm during the procedure. A special coil consisting of a radio-frequency transmitter is secured around the chest. This arrangement improves image quality by increasing radio signal strength, since the coil is located close to the tissue being examined. The imaging table is then moved inside a cylindrical magnetic scanning machine. A background magnetic field is used to align protons within the nuclei of hydrogen atoms in the heart tissue (hydrogen occurs abundantly in heart tissue in the form of water). The radio-frequency field (essentially a second magnetic field) is then pulsed on and off, causing the protons to change their orientation and thereby generating a signal that is detected by the scanner. These signals are converted into an image, and during a single session a doctor collects a series of images, often from several different angles. Cardiac MRI procedures typically last between 30 and 90 minutes. In some cases, to improve the visualization of the heart and its blood vessels, a patient may receive an intravenous injection with a contrast agent such as gadolinium.

Cardiac MRI is sometimes employed for stress testing, in which heart rate or blood flow to the heart is increased artificially through drug administration in order to detect obstructions in the coronary arteries or other heart vessels. In persons with coronary heart disease, cardiac MRI may be used to predict heart function prior to angioplasty or coronary artery bypass. In patients who have undergone these procedures, cardiac MRI can be used as a form of surveillance for signs of disease progression, including restenosis (the return of artery blockages). Although there are relatively few risks associated with cardiac MRI, the procedure can interfere with the function of metallic implants such as pacemakers, and some persons experience allergic reactions upon exposure to contrast agents.

INVASIVE EVALUATION TECHNIQUES

Invasive cardiovascular evaluation techniques involve the insertion of a catheter or other device into the patient's body. These procedures are most commonly used to investigate arteries to determine whether a particular vessel is occluded (blocked). Thus, invasive techniques are most frequently employed in the diagnosis, evaluation, and treatment of conditions such as atherosclerosis and coronary artery disease.

CARDIAC CATHETERIZATION

Cardiac catheterization is a medical procedure by which a flexible plastic tube (catheter) is inserted into an artery or vein. It is used for injecting drugs for therapy or diagnosis, for measuring blood flow and pressure in the heart and central blood vessels, in performing procedures such as angiography (X-ray examination of the arteries and veins) and angioplasty (a procedure used to dilate obstructed arteries), and as a means of passing electrodes into the heart to study, restore, or regulate the heartbeat. Catheterization is central to the diagnosis, therapy, and surgical management of many forms of cardiovascular disease.

The term *cardiac catheterization* was coined in 1844 by French physiologist Claude Bernard, who inserted a glass catheter into the heart of a horse. The procedure was first performed in a human by German physician Werner Forssmann, who in 1929 opened a vein in his own arm, inserted a urethral catheter about 3.2 mm (0.125 inch) in diameter and 76 cm (2.5 feet) long, and passed it to the right side of his heart while photographing his accomplishment with an X-ray machine. In the United States, physiologists André Cournand and Dickinson Richards developed clinical applications of Forssmann's technique, and in 1956 the three shared a Nobel Prize for their achievements.

Catheter materials and construction are very sophisticated, permitting an enormous range of diagnostic and therapeutic techniques to be applied to almost every organ and blood vessel in the body—but especially to the heart. By the 1940s catheters were being placed safely in the right chambers of the heart through veins, and by the 1950s they were being placed in the left chambers through arteries. As these techniques were developed, it became possible to monitor blood pressure and flow in medical and surgical intensive-care units. Through the ability to place one or more catheters inside the heart chambers, all types of heart abnormalities were opened to study.

Today, iodine contrast medium can be injected through the catheter into veins or directly into the heart chambers (angiography). This makes it possible to diagnose and surgically correct many heart conditions, including congenital heart abnormalities. In addition, visualization with a contrast agent enables the identification and replacement or repair of damaged heart valves and blood vessels and even the complete replacement of the heart through transplantation. The injection of contrast medium is particularly valuable in evaluating coronary artery narrowing and is usually performed to quantify the severity of disease present and to establish whether the person is a candidate for surgical intervention with balloon angioplasty or coronary bypass surgery. It is also used to evaluate patients with angina pectoris who do not respond to treatment.

Special catheterization techniques now permit a cardiologist to study the function and pathology of arterial walls. One notable technique is intravascular ultrasound, in which a tiny ultrasound transducer mounted on the tip of a cardiac catheter is used to generate images of the interior walls of coronary arteries.

ANGIOCARDIOGRAPHY

Angiocardiography is a method of following the passage of blood through the heart and great vessels by means of the intravenous injection of a radiopaque fluid, whose passage is followed by serialized X-ray pictures. In this procedure, a thin catheter is positioned into a heart chamber by inserting it into an artery, usually in the arm, threading it through the vessel around the shoulder, across the chest, and into the aorta. The radiopaque dye is then injected through the catheter. With the use of an X-ray, the dye can be seen to flow easily through the healthy sections but narrows to a trickle or becomes completely pinched off where lesions, such as fatty deposits, line and obstruct the lumen of blood vessels (characteristic of atherosclerosis). The most frequently used angiocardiographic methods are biplane angiocardiography and cineangiocardiography. In the first method, large X-ray films are exposed at the rate of 10 to 12 per second in two planes at right angles to each other, thus permitting the simultaneous recording of two different views.

In cineangiocardiography, the X-ray images are brightened several thousandfold with photoamplifiers and photographed on motion-picture films at speeds of up to 64 frames per second. When projected at 16 to 20 frames per second, the passage of the opacified blood may be viewed in slow motion.

Angiocardiography is used to evaluate patients for cardiovascular surgery. Although it is a valuable tool in assessing some of the more complicated aspects of heart function, it is also one of the most hazardous of all diagnostic procedures. Serious reactions to the iodine-containing compounds used, including radiopaque media, are not infrequent, despite continued efforts to develop less harmful materials.

ANGIOGRAPHY

Angiography, or arteriography, is a diagnostic imaging procedure in which arteries and veins are examined by using a contrast agent and X-ray technology. Blood vessels cannot be differentiated from the surrounding organs in conventional radiography. It is therefore necessary to inject into the lumen of the vessels a substance that will distinguish them from the surrounding tissues. The contrast medium used is a water-soluble substance containing iodine. On the radiograph, iodine-containing structures cast a denser shadow than do other body tissues. The technique in use today was developed in the early 1950s by Swedish cardiologist Sven-Ivar Seldinger.

In a typical angiography procedure, a needle is used to puncture the main artery in the groin, armpit, or crook of the arm and to place a coiled wire in the artery. The needle is withdrawn, and a small catheter is passed over the wire and into the artery. The wire is removed, and contrast medium is injected through the catheter. Both the arteries and the structures they supply with blood can then be visualized.

A technique called digital subtraction angiography (DSA) is particularly useful in diagnosing arterial occlusion. For example, it can be used to identify constriction (stenosis) of the carotid artery or clot formation (thrombosis) in a pulmonary artery. It also can be used to detect renal vascular disease. After contrast material is injected into an artery or vein, a physician produces fluoroscopic images. Using these digitized images, a computer subtracts the image made with contrast material from a postinjection image made without contrast material, producing an image that allows the dye in the arteries to be seen more clearly. In this manner, the images arising from soft tissues, bones, and gas are the same in both the initial and the subsequent image and are thereby eliminated by the subtraction process. The remaining images of blood vessels containing the contrast material are thus more prominent.

All organs of the body can be examined by using various angiography techniques. Radiographic evaluations of diseased arteries supplying the legs, the brain, and the heart are necessary before corrective surgical procedures are undertaken.

SURGICAL AND EMERGENCY CARDIAC TREATMENTS

Surgical treatments for cardiovascular disease include any procedure in which an incision is made into the heart or into a heart vessel. Open-heart surgery is perhaps the most complex type of the cardiovascular surgery, since it often requires cardiopulmonary bypass (the rerouting of a patient's blood through a heart-lung machine) in order to maintain circulation during the operation. Heart surgeries and emergency cardiac treatments are important life-saving procedures.

OPEN-HEART SURGERY

Open-heart surgery is any procedure that requires an incision into the heart, thus exposing one or more of the cardiac chambers, or requires the use of a heart-lung machine, a device that allows circulation and oxygenation of the blood to be maintained outside the patient's body. The most-common open-heart procedures are for repair of valvular disease and for correction of congenital heart defects, chiefly septal and valve defects. Open-heart surgery has also been used in the treatment of severe coronary artery disease.

CARDIOPULMONARY BYPASS

Cardiopulmonary bypass serves as a temporary substitute for a patient's heart and lungs during the course of open-heart surgery. The patient's blood is pumped through a heart-lung machine for artificial introduction of oxygen and removal of carbon dioxide. The use of a heart-lung machine during open-heart surgery allows the surgeon to access a dry and motionless heart.

Until the first such cardiopulmonary bypass devices were developed, most cases of valve disease and congenital defects either were considered inoperable or were corrected by "blind" (closed-heart) procedures. Before its first successful application to operations on the human heart in the early 1950s, all heart operations had to be done either by the sense of touch or with the heart open to view but with the patient's whole body held to a subnormal temperature (hypothermia). The latter procedure was feasible only for very brief periods (less than five minutes).

The first successful clinical use of a heart-lung machine was reported by American surgeon John H. Gibbon, Jr., in 1953. During this operation for the surgical closure of an atrial septal defect, cardiopulmonary bypass was achieved by a machine equipped with an oxygenator developed by Gibbon and a roller pump developed in 1932 by U.S. surgeon Michael E. DeBakey. The heart-lung machine proved highly valuable for open-heart surgery because the blood bypasses the heart and lungs, giving the surgeon an unobstructed view of the operative field. Since 1953, heart-lung machines have been greatly improved with smaller and more-efficient oxygenators, allowing them to be used not only in adults but also in children and even newborn infants.

Cardiopulmonary bypass is accomplished by use of large catheters inserted in the superior and inferior venae cavae, the large veins that return the blood from the systemic circulation to the right upper chamber of the heart. The deoxygenated blood returning to the heart from the upper and lower portions of the body enters these tubes and by gravity drainage flows into a collecting reservoir on the heart-lung machine. Blood then flows into an oxygenator, the lung component of the machine, where it is exposed to an oxygen-containing gas mixture or oxygen alone. In this manner, oxygen is introduced into the blood, and carbon dioxide is removed in sufficient quantities to make the blood leaving the oxygenator similar to that normally returning to the heart from the lungs.

From the oxygenator, blood is pumped back to the body and returned to the arterial tree through a cannula

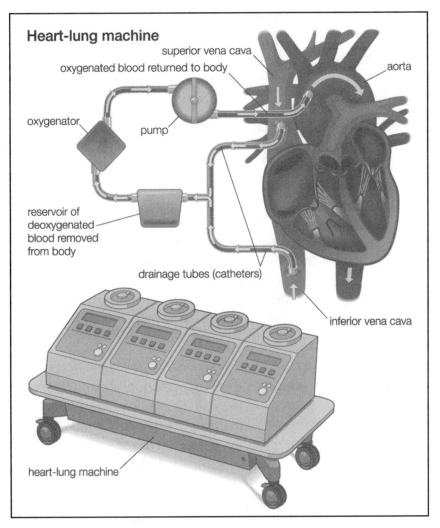

Heart-lung machine

superior vena cava

oxygenated blood returned to body

aorta

oxygenator

pump

reservoir of
deoxygenated
blood removed
from body

drainage tubes (catheters)

inferior vena cava

heart-lung machine

A heart-lung machine is connected to the heart by drainage tubes that divert blood from the venous system, directing it to an oxygenator. The oxygenator removes carbon dioxide and adds oxygen to the blood, which is then returned to the arterial system of the body. Encyclopædia Britannica, Inc.

(small tube) introduced in a major systemic artery, such as the femoral (groin) artery. The oxygenated blood pumped back into the patient's arteries is sufficient to maintain life at even the most distant parts of the body as well as in those organs with the greatest requirements (e.g., brain,

The Cardiovascular System

kidneys, and liver). To do this, up to 5 litres (1.3 gallons) or more of blood must be pumped each minute. While the heart is relieved of its pumping duties, it can be stopped, and the surgeon can perform open-heart surgery that may include valve repair or replacement, repair of defects inside the heart, or revascularization of blocked arteries.

The assemblage and sterilization of the components of the heart-lung machine are essential considerations, because the blood comes in contact with the apparatus outside of the body. Heart-lung machines have disposable tubing and plastic bubble oxygenators. Cardiopulmonary bypass is now more often carried out by using cardioplegic solutions designed to provide the heart with the necessary minimal nutrient and electrolyte requirements. Blood is also needed, and administration of an anticoagulant (heparin) prevents clotting of the blood while it is circulating in the heart-lung machine.

Mechanical Hearts

Mechanical hearts, which include total artificial hearts and ventricular assist devices (VADs), are machines that are capable of replacing or assisting the pumping action of the heart for prolonged periods without causing excessive damage to the blood components. Implantation of a total artificial heart requires removal of both of the patient's ventricles (lower chambers). However, with the use of a VAD to support either the right or the left ventricle, the entire heart remains in the body.

Mechanical hearts are implanted only after maximal medical management has failed. They may be used for cardiac resuscitation after cardiac arrest, for recovery from cardiogenic shock after heart surgery, and in some patients with chronic heart failure who are waiting for a heart transplant. Occasionally, mechanical hearts have

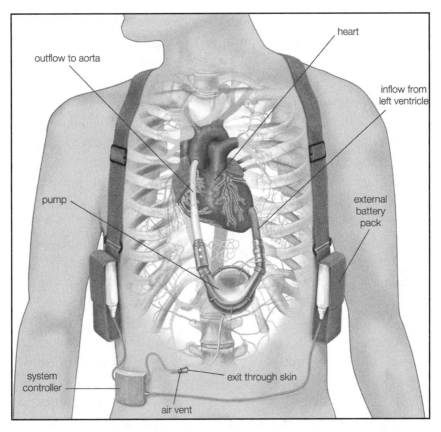

Ventricular assist device (VAD), a type of artificial heart designed to assist one of the ventricles (in this case the left) in pumping oxygenated blood through the aorta and to the body's tissues. The pump is placed inside the chest cavity, while the power source and system controller are carried on a harness outside the body. Encyclopædia Britannica, Inc.

been used as a permanent support in patients who do not qualify for a heart transplant or as a bridge to recovery of the patient's own diseased heart. The goal is to provide a safe, effective system that allows the recipient to move about freely, thus improving the quality of life. Some recipients of VADs have lived several years and have returned to work and normal physical activities.

A left VAD pumps oxygenated blood from the left ventricle to the aorta. The pumping part of the device is implanted in the left upper abdomen or left side of the chest. A tube from the pump exits the skin and connects to a controller that regulates the function of the pump and to a power source. Pneumatic devices have membranes or sacs that are moved by air pressure to pump the blood, while electrical devices use electromechanical systems for power. Electrical devices are being developed that are totally implantable and do not require a tube exiting the skin. With these devices, power to the pump is transmitted between external and internal batteries through the intact skin.

Most mechanical hearts incorporate various centrifugal pumps, paracorporeal pulsatile pumps, cardiopulmonary bypass (CPB) pumps, and the intra-aortic balloon pump (IABP). These pumps generate a pulsatile blood flow and pressure similar to those of the natural heart. Smaller devices known as axial flow pumps, on the other hand, generate continuous blood flow by a jet-engine type of technology. An experienced surgical team chooses the particular device to be implanted by assessing the patient's size, the amount of support the heart requires, and the expected duration of support.

The first successful use of a mechanical heart in a human was performed by Michael E. DeBakey in 1966. After surgery to replace the patient's aorta and mitral valve, a left VAD was installed, making it possible to wean the patient from the heart-lung machine. After 10 days of pump flow from the VAD, the heart recovered, and the VAD was removed. During the 1970s synthetic materials were developed that greatly aided the development of permanent artificial hearts. One such device, designed by American physician Robert K. Jarvik, was surgically implanted into a patient by American surgeon William C. DeVries in 1982. The aluminum and plastic device, called the Jarvik-7 for its inventor, replaced the patient's two ventricles. Two rubber diaphragms, designed to mimic the pumping action of the natural heart, were kept beating by an external compressor that was connected to the implant by hoses. This first recipient survived 112 days and died as a result of various physical complications caused by the implant. Subsequent patients fared little better or even worse, so that use of the Jarvik-7 was stopped. In 2001 a team of American surgeons implanted the first completely self-contained artificial heart, called the AbioCor artificial heart. The patient survived 151 days.

In 2008 a fully functional artificial heart was developed by Carmat, a French company founded by cardiologist Alain Carpentier. The device was covered with a specially designed biosynthetic material to prevent the development of blood clots and to reduce the likelihood of immune rejection—problems associated with the AbioCor and Jarvik-7 artificial hearts. The Carmat heart also utilized sensors to regulate blood flow and heartbeat. Plans to test the heart first in calves and sheep and later in humans with terminal heart failure were being developed.

VALVULAR AND PERICARDIAL SURGERIES

Destroyed heart valves can be replaced with artificial valves (prostheses) made of stainless steel, Dacron™, or other special materials. The heart-lung machine is used during these operations, in which one, two, or even three cardiac valves may be removed and replaced with the appropriate artificial valve. The use of both homograft valves (obtained from human beings after death) and heterograft valves (secured from animals) is widespread. One of the advantages of both types is the absence of clotting, which occurs occasionally with the use of artificial valves. Most homograft and heterograft valves have a durability of 10–15 years. There is a risk of endocarditis with all types of valves.

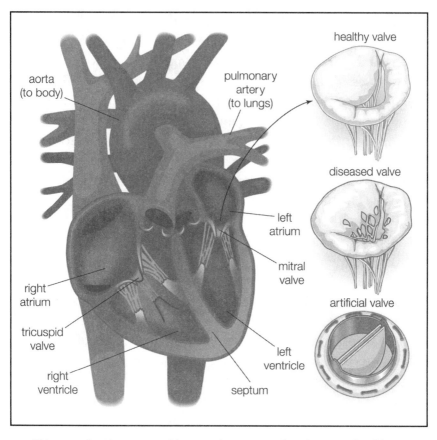

Diagram showing a normal heart valve compared with an artificial heart valve. Encyclopædia Britannica, Inc.

Chronic constrictive pericarditis can affect the surface of the heart and the sac (pericardium) surrounding it. The pericardium becomes thickened and fibrotic, and over a period of time it constricts the heart so that the normal filling of the ventricles during the resting phase of the cardiac cycle is limited. This condition in turn reduces the output of the heart and eventually affects all the organ systems, including the brain, liver, and kidneys. Treatment is the surgical removal of the thickened pericardium around the heart, which permits normal filling and expansion of the ventricles and restores adequate cardiac output to the vital organs.

CARDIAC PACEMAKERS

A pacemaker is an electronic cardiac-support device that produces rhythmic electrical impulses that take over the regulation of the heartbeat in patients with certain types of heart disease. A healthy human heart contains its own electrical conducting system capable of controlling both the rate and the order of cardiac contractions. Electrical impulses are generated at the sinoatrial node in the right atrium. They then pass through the muscles of both atria to trigger the contraction of those two chambers, which forces blood into the ventricles. The wave of atrial electrical activity activates a second patch of conductive tissue, the atrioventricular node, initiating a second discharge along an assembly of conductive fibres called the bundle of His, which induces the contraction of the ventricles. When electrical conduction through the atrioventricular node or bundle of His is interrupted, the condition is called heart block. An artificial pacemaker may be employed temporarily until normal conduction returns or permanently to overcome the block.

In temporary pacing, a miniature electrode attached to fine wires is introduced into the heart through a vein, usually in the arm. The pacing device, an electric generator, remains outside the body and produces regular pulses of electric charge to maintain the heartbeat. In permanent pacing, the electrode may again be passed into the heart through a vein or it may be surgically implanted on the surface of the heart. In either case the electrode is generally located in the right ventricle. The electric generator is placed just beneath the skin, usually in a surgically created pocket below the collarbone.

The first pacemakers were of a type called asynchronous, or fixed, and they generated regular discharges that over-rode the natural pacemaker. The rate of an asynchronous pacemaker may be altered by the physician, but once set it will continue to generate an electric pulse at regular intervals. Most are set at 70 to 75 beats per minute. More-recent devices are synchronous, or demand, pacemakers that trigger heart contractions only when the normal beat is interrupted. Most pacemakers of this type are designed to generate a pulse when the natural heart rate falls below 68 to 72 beats per minute.

Once in place, the electrode and wires of the pacemaker usually require almost no further attention. The power source of the implanted pulse generator, however, requires replacement at regular intervals, generally every four to five years. Most pacemakers use batteries as a power source.

Pacemakers designed to communicate wirelessly, using radio-frequency telemetry-based technology, have enabled physicians to gather information about a patient remotely. The implanted pacemakers transmit information to home monitoring systems and to programming devices used by doctors. As a result, a doctor working in a clinic can collect important information about a patient's heart function while the patient is at home. This type of wireless device also sends out alert signals to the physician when the patient's heart rate becomes abnormal.

REPAIR OF HEART WOUNDS

Heart wounds are caused by blunt or penetrating instru-ments. The rapid deceleration often experienced in automobile accidents is a common cause of injury to the heart muscle, resulting in bruising and even disruption of a valve or the ventricular septum. Both bullet and stab wounds account for many patients treated in the emergency clinics of major hospitals. Prompt diagnosis and effective surgical treatment, usually consisting of control of bleeding by sewing the heart muscle at the point of entry of the foreign object, have resulted in a high rate of successful treatment.

CORONARY ARTERY BYPASS SURGERY

Coronary artery bypass surgery is used to restore adequate blood flow to the heart muscle beyond severe atheromatous obstruction in the main coronary arteries. Coronary artery bypass surgery entails transplanting one or more veins to create new paths for arterial blood to flow from the aorta through the coronary arteries, circumventing the obstructed sections of the arteries. Coronary artery bypass surgery became widely used after its safety and usefulness in relieving the pain of angina were demonstrated in the late 1960s.

The grafts used in coronary artery bypass surgery are usually saphenous veins taken from one or both of the patient's legs. Multiple grafts are often used for multiple atheromatous occlusions. In the case of double bypass surgery one of the internal mammary arteries, which supply blood to the chest wall, can be diverted to supply the heart muscle. However, since there are only two internal mammary arteries, their use is limited.

There are two principal uses for coronary artery bypass surgery. One is to relieve chest angina that is resistant to medication. The other is to prolong a person's life; however, this is only achieved when all three main coronary arteries are severely obstructed and when the contractility of the left ventricle has been impaired somewhat. Coronary artery bypass surgery does not prolong life when it is used to overcome an obstruction in only one or even two arteries. As a nonsurgical option, coronary angioplasty is also used to unblock arteries.

ANGIOPLASTY

The development of catheters with strong inflatable balloons constructed toward their end and along the line of the catheter has greatly changed cardiac surgery. The balloons can be inflated by compressed air at different controlled pressures. They are used for dilation of a partly obstructed coronary artery (percutaneous transluminal coronary angioplasty, or PTCA), with restoration of blood flow to the heart muscle, and of a severely obstructed heart valve, particularly the aortic valve, relieving the pressure on the left ventricle.

The procedure generally requires no anesthetic and, by using specialized radiological imaging techniques, is

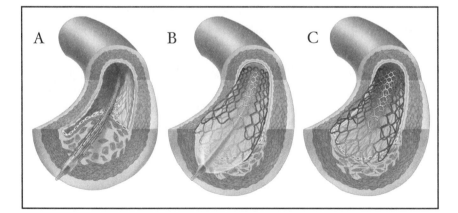

(A) In a coronary artery where blood flow is obstructed by the growth of an atherosclerotic plaque, the point of obstruction is reached by a cardiac catheter encased in an inflatable balloon and wire-mesh stent. (B) The balloon is inflated, thus expanding the stent, dilating the artery, and compressing the plaque. (C) The balloon is deflated and withdrawn with the catheter, leaving the stent expanded against the arterial wall. Encyclopædia Britannica, Inc.

sometimes done on an outpatient basis. Several coronary arteries may be dilated in this way, with flattening of the atheromatous material against and into the arterial wall. Although there are operative risks, such as emboli and tearing, the results are excellent, and the technique may be repeated if necessary. However, the use of drug-coated stents has decreased the need for repeat angioplasty.

HEART TRANSPLANTATION

Heart transplantation is a medical procedure involving the removal of a diseased heart from a patient and its replacement with a healthy heart. Because of the immense complexity of the procedure and the difficulty of finding appropriate donors, heart transplants are performed only as a last resort in patients with end-stage heart failure or irreparable heart damage whose projected survival with their own heart is only a few weeks or months. In most cases, transplanted hearts are taken from persons who have suffered irreversible brain damage and have been declared legally dead but whose organs have been kept artificially viable for the purposes of transplant.

The first heart transplant in an experimental model was performed by French surgeon Alexis Carrel in 1905. American surgeon Norman Shumway achieved the first successful heart transplant in a dog in 1958. In 1967, South African surgeon Christiaan Barnard performed the first human heart transplant. His success was followed by attempts at many other medical centres, but lack of adequate therapy to combat immune rejection of the transplanted heart led most surgeons to abandon the procedure after the initial attempts. Barnard, Shumway, and some others, however, continued to perform heart transplants, and in the 1970s cyclosporine, a compound isolated from an earth fungus, was discovered to be a very effective drug for combating rejection. Cyclosporine brought about a rapid and successful increase in the number of heart transplant procedures. The survival rate at one year is now about 84 percent and at three years about 77 percent. Many heart transplant patients are able to lead productive lives for years after the procedure.

Heart transplant actually occurs in several stages. First comes the selection and care of the transplant candidate. Patients with end-stage heart failure are acutely ill and require extraordinary support, often including mechanical circulatory assistance or the placement of devices that support the circulation. The second stage is the harvesting of the donor heart (frequently at a remote site) and timely implantation of the heart in the recipient. Both processes mount significant challenges. Current implantation procedure involves removal of the diseased heart except for some of the tissue from the atria, the two upper chambers of the heart. Leaving this tissue in place preserves nerve connections to the sinoatrial node, a patch of electroconductive tissue that regulates heartbeat. The replacement heart is removed from the donor and preserved in a cold salt solution. During implantation it is trimmed to fit and sutured into place, making all necessary vascular connections.

The third stage of heart transplant is the postoperative period, which is directed toward providing adequate antirejection treatment with close monitoring to prevent rejection of the heart. Medical therapy "trains" the immune system to cope with a foreign heart, but patients require lifelong immune suppression. Indeed, a successful transplant is very demanding on the patient and requires close follow-up, especially during the first year, to decrease the risk of rejection and prevent infections associated with immune suppression. Partly for this reason, it is an extraordinary option for those who are very ill and have no other alternative. Heart transplant is not a cure for heart failure but is a new condition in which the recipient gains new life and functional capacity, though with the commitment to maintain lifelong medical treatment to prevent rejection and infection.

CARDIOPULMONARY RESUSCITATION

Cardiopulmonary resuscitation, or CPR, is an emergency procedure for providing artificial respiration and blood circulation when normal breathing and circulation have stopped, usually as a result of trauma such as heart attack or near drowning. CPR buys time for the trauma victim by supplying life-sustaining oxygen to the brain and other vital organs until fully equipped emergency medical personnel arrive on the scene.

While training is required for conventional CPR, a modern form, known as "hands-only" CPR, may be performed by individuals who have not received formal training. According to the American Heart Association (AHA), hands-only CPR, which is recommended solely for use on adults who have suddenly collapsed, requires just "two steps to save a life." First, the person who acts (the rescuer) takes steps to summon emergency medical personnel to the scene. Second, the rescuer begins to push hard and fast in the centre of the victim's chest, forcing the chest down 4–5 cm (1.5–2 inches) with each press. Chest presses should continue uninterrupted, at a rate of 100 presses per minute, until medical personnel arrive. Hands-only CPR performed on adults who have suddenly collapsed is just as effective as conventional CPR. However, the AHA recommends only conventional CPR be used on children and infants.

The first step in conventional CPR is to establish unconsciousness. If the victim is unconscious, the rescuer summons help and then prepares to administer CPR. The sequence of steps may be summarized as the ABCs of CPR—*A* referring to *airway*, *B* to *breathing*, and *C* to *circulation*.

The rescuer opens the victim's airway by placing him on his back, tilting the head back, and lifting the chin. Then the rescuer should check for signs of breathing.

If the victim is not breathing, the rescuer must perform mouth-to-mouth resuscitation. In this procedure he makes an airtight seal with his mouth over the victim's mouth while at the same time pinching the victim's nostrils shut. The rescuer breathes twice into the victim's mouth, causing the victim's chest to rise visibly each time and allowing it to deflate naturally. Artificial respiration is performed at a rate of about 12 times per minute.

The rescuer next looks for signs of circulation. The recommended method is to check for a pulse in the carotid artery of the neck. If a pulse is not felt after 10 seconds of careful searching, the rescuer proceeds to deliver chest compressions. The rescuer places the heels of his hands, overlapping, on the lower half of the victim's breastbone, or sternum. With his elbows locked, arms straight, and shoulders directly over the victim, the rescuer uses his upper body to apply a perpendicularly directed force onto the victim's sternum. The chest is depressed approximately 4–5 cm (1.5–2 inches) at a brisk rate of about 100 compressions per minute. At the end of each compression, pressure is released and the chest allowed to rebound completely, though the rescuer's hands are not removed. After 30 compressions, the rescuer delivers two full breaths, then another 30 compressions, and so on. CPR continues uninterrupted until spontaneous breathing and circulation are restored or until professional medical assistance is obtained. The procedure is modified somewhat for infants and children and under special circumstances (such as multiple injuries).

Before the introduction of modern CPR techniques, attempts to revive victims of cardiac or respiratory arrest were sporadic and rarely successful. In 1958 Peter Safar and James Elam, anesthesiologists at Johns Hopkins Hospital in Baltimore, Md., described an emergency ventilation technique that involved tipping the victim's head back and pulling the jaw forward in order to clear the air passage and then blowing air into the victim's lungs through a mouth-to-mouth connection. Safar's technique was the basis of what became the first two letters (for *airway* and *breathing*) in the ABCs of CPR. The basis of the third letter (for *circulation*) was provided by electrical engineer William B. Kouwenhoven and colleagues, also at Johns Hopkins, who in 1960 described the "closed-chest cardiac massage," a method of restoring circulation in a heart-attack victim by pushing down rhythmically on the sternum. The combination of Kouwenhoven's technique with Safar's ventilation technique evolved into the basic method of CPR. In the mid-1990s a group of researchers at the University of Arizona Sarver Heart Center discovered that continual chest presses kept blood circulating in adult victims of cardiac arrest better than conventional CPR techniques. They found that mouth-to-mouth breaths required too much time, resulting in slowed or stopped circulation before compressions were resumed. In 2008 the researchers' "hands-only" method for adult victims, which uses only continuous chest presses, was adopted by the AHA.

DEFIBRILLATION

Defibrillation is the administration of electric shocks to the heart in order to reset normal heart rhythm in persons who are experiencing cardiac arrest or whose heart function is endangered because of severe arrhythmia (abnormality of heart rhythm).

Types of Defibrillation Devices

There are several different kinds of defibrillation devices. The two major types are automated external defibrillators (AEDs) and automatic implantable cardioverter defibrillators (ICDs). AEDs are used in emergency situations involving cardiac arrest. They are portable and often can be found in places where large numbers of people circulate, such as in airports. Immediate emergency response that enables early defibrillation is central to the successful restoration of heart rhythm during cardiac arrest. Emergency personnel are trained in the use of AEDs. However, AEDs are designed to be used by members of the general public as well, regardless of training. Many countries that supply AEDs in public areas offer training courses, often in conjunction with training in CPR (cardiopulmonary resuscitation).

ICDs are used in patients at high risk of sustained or recurrent arrhythmia that has the potential to impair heart function. An ICD consists of a shock generator and wires with electrodes on both ends. The generator is implanted under the skin in the chest or abdomen and is connected to the wires, which are fed through a major vein to reach the atria or ventricles of the heart. When a disturbance in rhythm is detected by the ICD, it delivers an electric shock to the heart to reestablish normal rhythm. This is known as cardioversion. When heart rhythm becomes chaotic, the ICD delivers a shock that resets the rhythm, thereby performing the function of defibrillation. Cardioversion and defibrillation have enabled ICDs to prevent sudden death in some patients affected by severe ventricular arrhythmias. ICDs can be programmed to perform other functions, including slowing heart rhythm in persons with tachycardia (abnormally fast heart rate) and increasing heart rhythm in persons with bradycardia (abnormally slow heart rate).

History of Defibrillation

Defibrillation has long been recognized to be a lifesaving procedure. One of the first reported incidents in which electricity was used for the resuscitation of an apparently dead individual occurred in England in 1774, when electric shocks applied to the thorax of a young girl reestablished her pulse. In the 1780s British surgeon Charles Kite invented a precursor of the modern defibrillation device, and later studies, including those conducted by Italian physician and physicist Luigi Galvani in the 1790s and by Italian physicist Carlo Matteucci in the 1840s, shed light on the electrical properties of animal tissues. In fact, Matteucci, in his studies of electricity detection in pigeons, was the first to detect an electrical current in the heart. Research performed in the following decades led to an improved understanding of the electrical features of heart rhythm.

In 1947 American physician Claude S. Beck, who had been investigating new techniques for defibrillation in humans, reported having successfully reestablished normal heart rhythm in a patient with ventricular fibrillation (irregular and uncoordinated contraction of the ventricle muscle fibres) while performing heart surgery. Beck's defibrillation technique and device served as a prototype for the development of modern defibrillators. In the 1960s Polish-born U.S. physician Michel Mirowski came up with an idea for the development of an automatic implantable cardioverter defibrillator, which could be used in patients affected by certain types of arrhythmia. The first ICD was implanted in a patient on Feb. 4, 1980.

Emergency personnel were trained in defibrillation beginning in the 1960s, and the first automated external defibrillator devices were clinically tested in the early 1980s. The first AEDs delivered strong shocks in a monophasic waveform and often required multiple shocks to reestablish heart rhythm. Later AEDs were refined to deliver shocks in a biphasic waveform, which, relative to monophasic shock, was found to be safer and more effective.

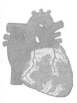

CONCLUSION

Cardiology and understanding of the cardiovascular system and of cardiovascular disease has continued to progress in the 21st century. Today, countless researchers across the globe are working to better understand the mechanisms underlying the pathology of cardiovascular disease, as well as to identify the causes, genetic and environmental, that contribute to the development of these conditions.

Efforts to develop more precise imaging techniques and other valuable cardiovascular evaluation procedures are ongoing. As existing technologies are refined and new technologies emerge, the diagnosis of cardiovascular disease promises to become increasingly precise. In addition, pharmacologists are working to develop new drugs capable of treating heart and blood vessel diseases. These efforts, in combination with continuous improvements in scientists' understanding of the mechanisms controlling cardiovascular function, are poised to significantly advance the treatment of complex cardiovascular diseases in the coming decades.

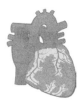
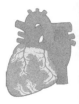

GLOSSARY

anastomosing Connecting the blood vessel branches so they can intercommunicate or work together. Can also refer to the surgical, traumatic, or pathological formation of an opening between two normally separate anatomical spaces.

azygous A single, unpaired vein.

depolarization The neutralization of polarity, or the reduction of a membrane potential to a more positive value. In many muscle cells and neurons, this process leads to an electric impulse called an action potential. In the heart, it can cause problems with the heart's ability to beat.

distensible Capable of being enlarged from internal pressure.

echocardiograms Visual records of the heart's structure made by high frequency sound waves that are directed at the heart and reflected back.

electrocardiograms Line graphs made by recording the electrical potential that happens during a heartbeat.

electrolytes Nonmetallic electronic conductors in which currents are carried by the movement of ions.

endothelial Relating to the single layer of flattened cells that line internal body cavities.

foramen ovale An opening in the septum between the two atria of the heart that is normally present only in the fetus.

hemiazygos vein A vein running superiorly in the lower thoracic region of the body, just to the left of the spinal column.

hypertrophy Increase in size of an organ; thickening of muscle fibers.

innominate artery A short artery that comes from the aortic arch and divides into the subclavian and carotid arteries of the right side.

lesions Abnormal changes in the structure of an organ or body part due to injury or disease.

lumen The cavity of a blood vessel or other tubular cavity.

perfuse To force a fluid through an organ or tissue, especially by way of the blood vessels.

piezoelectric Functioning by means of electricity or electric polarity due to pressure.

plasma The fluid part of the blood, as differentiated from the suspended material (i.e., red blood cells, white blood cells, platelets, etc.).

pulsatile Marked by rhythmic throbbing or vibrating, as in a blood vessel.

reticulum Any of a fine network, especially one in the body composed of blood vessels or cells.

sinoatrial node A small mass of tissue that is embedded in the musculature of the right atrium of higher vertebrates (such as humans) and that is responsible for creating the impulses that stimulate the heartbeat.

stenosis A narrowing or constricting of the diameter of a bodily passage.

subclavian Related to something, such as an artery or vein, that is under the clavicle, or collarbone.

sulci Fissures or grooves in an organ or tissue, especially those that mark the convolutions on the surface of the brain.

trabeculae carneae Protruding columns of muscle, round or irregular in shape, found along the inner surface of the heart's ventricle.

truncus arteriosus A heart defect in which a single blood vessel replaces the pulmonary artery and the aorta, which results in the mixing of oxygenated and deoxygenated blood.

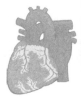

BIBLIOGRAPHY

General accounts and elementary descriptions of circulatory systems are found in many biology textbooks, including the following: Raymond F. Oram, *Biology: Living Systems*, 5th ed. (1986); Karen Arms and Pamela S. Camp, *Biology*, 3rd ed. (1986); and Paul B. Weisz and Richard N. Keogh, *The Science of Biology*, 5th ed. (1982). Textbooks dealing with animal structure at a more advanced level include the following: Ralph M. Buchsbaum, *Animals Without Backbones*, 3rd ed. (1987); Robert D. Barnes, *Invertebrate Zoology*, 5th ed. (1987); Alfred Sherwood Romer and Thomas S. Parsons, *The Vertebrate Body*, 6th ed. (1986); and Charles K. Weichert, *Anatomy of the Chordates*, 4th ed. (1970); Knut Schmidt-Nielsen, *Animal Physiology: Adaptation and Environment*, 3rd ed. (1983); and Milton Hildebrand, *Analysis of Vertebrate Structure*, 2nd ed. (1982).

For the history of circulation studies, see Helen Rapson, *The Circulation of Blood* (1982); David J. Furley and J.S. Wilkie (eds.), *Galen on Respiration and the Arteries* (1984); *The Selected Writings of William Gilbert, Galileo Galilei, William Harvey* (1952), in "The Great Books of the Western World" series; Fredrick A. Willius and Thomas J. Dry, *A History of the Heart and the Circulation* (1948); and Alfred P. Fishman and Dickinson W. Richards, *Circulation of the Blood: Men and Ideas* (1964, reprinted 1982). Special studies of circulation include Donald A. McDonald, *Blood Flow in Arteries*, 2nd ed. (1974); David I. Abramson and Philip B. Dobrin (eds.), *Blood Vessels and Lymphatics in Organ Systems* (1984); Colin L. Schwartz, Nicholas T. Werthessen, and Stewart Wolf, *Structure and Function of the Circulation*, 3 vol. (1980–81); and Jerry Franklin Green, *Fundamental Cardiovascular and Pulmonary Physiology*, 2nd ed. (1987).

Stanley W. Jacob, Clarice Ashworth Francone, and Walter J. Lossow, *Structure and Function in Man*, 5th ed. (1982), and Gary A. Thibodeau, *Anatomy and Physiology* (1987), are basic texts. Arthur C. Guyton, *Human Physiology and Mechanisms of Disease*, 4th ed. (1987), is a technical description of the physiology of cardiac muscle, heart function, and hemodynamics. Also see Peter F. Cohn, *Clinical Cardiovascular Physiology* (1985); James J. Smith and John P. Kampine, *Circulatory Physiology: The Essentials* (1984); Harvey V. Sparks, Jr., and Thom W. Rooke, *Essentials of Cardiovascular Physiology* (1987); and Peter Harris and Donald Heath, *The Human Pulmonary Circulation*, 3rd ed. (1986).

Coverage of the cardiovascular system and disease is provided in R. Wayne Alexander, Robert C. Schlant, and Valentin Fuster, *Hurst's the Heart*, 9th ed. (1998); Harry A. Fozzard et al. (eds.), *The Heart and Cardiovascular System: Scientific Foundations*, 2 vol. (1986); Wrynn Smith, *Cardiovascular Disease* (1987); Arthur J. Moss and Hugh D. Allen, *Moss and Adams' Heart Disease in Infants, Children, and Adolescents: Including the Fetus and Young Adult*, 7th ed. (2008); Robert H. Anderson et al. (eds.), *Paediatric Cardiology*, 2nd ed. (2001); Edward K. Chung (ed.), *Quick Reference to Cardiovascular Diseases*, 3rd ed. (1987); and Anders G. Olsson (ed.), *Atherosclerosis: Biology and Clinical Science* (1987).

Treatment and prevention of vascular problems are the subject of Joseph K. Perloff, *Physical Examination of the Heart and Circulation,* 3rd ed. (2000); and Peter Libby et al. (eds.), *Heart Disease: A Textbook of Cardiovascular Medicine*, 8th ed. (2008).

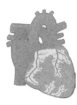

Index